Change in Focus

NICHOLAS LASH was born in 1934, educated at Downside and Oscott, and is a priest of the Northampton diocese. After several years of parish work, he moved to Cambridge, where he received his doctorate for a study of the methodology of Newman's *Essay on Development*. He is at present Fellow and Dean of St Edmund's House, Cambridge.

Author of *His Presence in the World* (Sheed & Ward, 1968), he has edited or contributed to a number of collections, including *Authority in a Changing Church* (Sheed & Ward, 1968); *The Christian Priesthood* (Darton, Longman & Todd, 1970); *Church Membership and Intercommunion* (Darton, Longman & Todd, 1973).

He is a member of the National Theology Commission for England and Wales, and of the editorial board of the 'Dogma' section of *Concilium*. He contributes regularly to a number of journals, including *New Blackfriars* and the *Irish Theological Quarterly*.

CHANGE IN FOCUS

A study of doctrinal change
and continuity

Nicholas Lash

Sheed and Ward · London

First published 1973
Sheed and Ward Ltd, 33 Maiden Lane, London WC2E 7LA
© Nicholas Lash 1973

Nihil obstat: John M. T. Barton *Censor*
Imprimatur: David Norris *Vicar General*
Westminster, 14 February 1973

This book is set in 11 on 12 pt 'Monotype' Baskerville type
Made and printed in Great Britain
by W & J Mackay Limited, Chatham

CONTENTS

For the Master and Fellows
St Edmund's House
Cambridge

INTRODUCTION

John Courtney Murray is said to have remarked that 'the question underlying all other questions treated at the Council was doctrinal development' (MacKinnon [1968] p 269). And a Dutch protestant scholar, in an essay originally written for a symposium marking the centenary of Darwin's *Origin of Species*, said of the problem of doctrinal evolution: 'The question at stake is whether and how we can prove that we are still the self-same Church' (Van Ruler [1961] p 91). The immediate difficulty facing someone who decides to write on the problem of change and continuity is that there is no aspect of christian belief, doctrine and activity which does not form part of, and is not increasingly *felt* to form part of, the problem. Therefore, where do we start, and how are we to tackle the job?

One way of tackling it would be to conduct a survey of the more significant contributions to catholic debates on doctrinal development during the past century and a half. But this has recently been done in Mark Schoof's admirable book, *Breakthrough* (cf Schoof [1970] pp 157–227). Another way would be to attempt a detailed, rigorously argued theoretical analysis of the problem, without burdening the text with references to the work of other theologians, living or dead. But although this method would have its advantages, the result might well seem not only excessively abstract, but also simply to be an expression of one individual's point of view.

A third approach, which in the end I decided to adopt in this book, offends against almost all the canons of respectable scholarship. This approach consists in trying to build up, inductively and cumulatively, an impression of the way in which the shape of the problem has changed in recent years. The result is, inevitably, a personal view, but I have tried to connect a wide range of topics, and the work of a number of different thinkers, past and present, in the hope that the reader—even if he does not come to see the problem in the way in which, in recent years, I have come to see it—would at least be provided with some materials on the basis of which he can go on to do the job much better for himself. Such an approach is inevitably unscholarly because an adequate exploration of any one of the themes or authors discussed would demand, in itself, a book at least as long as this one and would—in most cases—be beyond my competence. But I happen to believe that, in an age of increasing specialisation, the price that theologians sometimes pay for protecting their scholarly virtue is that too often they are not prepared to take the risk of making the connections. I have taken the risk, and must accept the consequences.

Once having decided to work in this impressionistic way, there could then be no question of conducting a single, linear argument—even chronologically. Instead, this book has four parts, in each of which the same themes and topics recur but, on each occasion, from a different point of view and in somewhat greater depth.

In the first part, we shall be concerned with the first two chapters of Vatican ii's *Constitution on Divine Revelation*. One of the advantages of starting with the text of *Dei Verbum* is that it provides us with a context in which such concepts as 'revelation', 'tradition', 'creed', 'dogma' and *'magisterium'*—all of which will concern us throughout the book—appear in some sort of coherent relationship.

The emphasis in the second group of chapters is historical. They include thumbnail sketches of the history of the concepts of 'tradition', 'creed', 'dogma' and (more selectively) *'magisterium'*.

The third part follows the development of doctrines of development from the middle of the nineteenth to the middle of the twentieth century. Here, rather than provide a general survey, I have preferred—for the most part—to concentrate on a few key figures from the catholic theology of that period, from Newman, Loisy and Blondel to de Lubac, Rahner, Schillebeeckx and Lonergan.

If there is a thesis argued in this book it is to the effect that, just as 'static' models of historical experience gave way to more 'dynamic' or 'evolutionary' conceptions of history during the nineteenth century, so the latter, in our own day, are being replaced by more concrete, episodic views of history in which

the 'situatedness' of the historian is taken more seriously, and
which allow for greater attention to be paid to problems of
historical discontinuity. And whereas theories of doctrinal
development or evolution were an appropriate theological
expression of the historical consciousness of the period that is
now coming to an end, they have become—in our own day—
increasingly unsatisfactory as conceptualisations of historical
understanding. Therefore, in the final group of chapters, I
have tried to suggest a framework within which the problems
that have concerned us throughout the book might appropriately be tackled today. In so doing, it has been necessary
to connect the theological debates with the way in which
similar methodological problems are being discussed in some
other disciplines.

Although the early chapters will seem very elementary to
anyone who has already studied the text of *Dei Verbum*, it is
to be hoped that, by situating the problems within a familiar
framework, they may help to make the later chapters less
indigestible. Be that as it may, I shall have done what I set
but to do if anyone who reads the book finds that he has a
clearer view of the problems by the end than he had at the
beginning. We are, I believe, privileged to be living at a time
of profound cultural crisis. Privileged, because the nature of
the times in which we live puts a particular burden of responsibility upon the choices that we make for the future. In a
situation such as ours, it would be illusory to suppose that
anyone has 'the answers'. It is enough for a pilgrim people,
and it is no small thing, if we succeed in asking the right
questions.

NICHOLAS LASH
Cambridge
1973

ACKNOWLEDGEMENTS

During the summer of 1970, I gave a course of lectures on problems of doctrinal development, in the University of Notre Dame, Indiana. It would be most unfair on my students to blame them for this book but, if they had not been as kind and encouraging as they were, I probably would not have settled down, two years later, to expand those lectures into this book. While I have tried to bring the material up to date, the structure of the book still, deliberately, reflects its origins.

The texts of the Vatican Council are taken from *The Documents of Vatican* II ed Walter Abbot, SJ, published by Geoffrey Chapman, London and Dublin, 1966.

PART ONE

THE CONSTITUTION ON DIVINE REVELATION

HISTORY OF THE CONSTITUTION

'There is a respectable theological view that, outstanding as is the importance of the much larger dogmatic Constitution on the Church, the Constitution on Divine Revelation may prove to be the supreme achievement of this council' (Butler, B. C. [1967] p 28). We may regard it as providential that this is so, because the problems with which this *Constitution* was concerned are increasingly being recognised as being among the most fundamental problems for contemporary christian belief and doctrine.

It is not my intention to add yet another item to the long list of commentaries on *Dei Verbum* that have been published in recent years. I shall restrict myself to those aspects of the *Constitution* which bear most directly upon the themes and problems with which this book is concerned. Moreover, by considering only this one *Constitution*, it will not even be possible to present 'the teaching of Vatican II' on these themes and problems. In order to do that, it would be necessary to examine several other documents promulgated by the council: the *Constitution on the Church*, for its discussion of the nature and function of the *magisterium*; the *Decree on Ecumenism*, for the idea that there is a 'hierarchy of doctrines'; the *Constitution on the Church in the World of Today*, for its treatment of the relationship between the church and the societies and cultures in which it lives and seeks to exercise its mission; and so on. Nevertheless, even within the narrow terms of reference that I have set myself, an examination of the *Constitution on Revelation* should provide a useful context within which to indicate some of the questions which we shall look at in more detail in subsequent parts of the book.

'A conciliar document must be interpreted in the light of its historical development at the Council' (Baum [1967] p 51). That should be obvious, and yet 'It is typical for our Roman Catholic mentality that we easily tolerate a large amount of critical hermeneutical studies on the Bible, and we even do possess papal and conciliar documents approving this kind of approach, but that it does not seem to be accepted in our Church to risk establishing the proper hermeneutical rules for the interpretation of the Church's documents. This curious anomaly in our attitude, which necessarily reveals a remarkable vulnerability and one-sidedness in our mentality, allows for a greater reverence towards the Church's statements than towards the doctrine of the Bible, the Word of God' (Fransen [1972] p 4). It is quite inadequate, therefore, simply to open the text of a conciliar document, and 'see what it says'. We must try to situate it in the historical context of the debates from which it emerged. Only in this way can we hope to discover what is important and what is unimportant; what was simply taken for granted, and what was the fruit of critical examination and vigorous debate; what were its achievements, and what its failures.

In these four chapters we shall, firstly, make some remarks about the successive drafts of the *Constitution*: secondly, look briefly at the notion of 'revelation' which it contains; thirdly, try to establish where it stands on the problem of scripture and tradition; and, fourthly, say something about its treatment of the problem of 'doctrinal development' itself, and about the role of the *magisterium* in the believing community's hearing of and response to the word of God.

The subject of revelation 'spanned practically the whole course of the council' (Butler B. C. [1967] p 28). The first draft was presented to the first session in November 1962, and the fifth and final version was approved, during the fourth session, on 29 November 1965. It is thus hardly surprising that the changes which the text underwent, in successive drafts, reflect the development of the mind of the council.

Each version had chapters on the old testament, the new testament, and on 'Holy Scripture in the Life of the Church'.[1] These chapters will not directly concern us, but it should be borne in mind that their successive drafts were increasingly marked by an openness to modern biblical scholarship in their description of inspiration and of methods of exegesis (cf Tavard [1966] p 7).

The original draft of the *Constitution* was entitled 'On the Sources of Revelation', and its first two chapters were 'The Double Source of Revelation', and 'The Inspiration, Inerrancy and Literary Form of Scripture' (Tavard [1966] p 3). This draft was preoccupied with the problem of scripture and tradition which, in the preparatory stages before the council opened had, significantly, been consigned to a chapter on the *magisterium* in a draft document on the church, prepared in 1960 (cf Van Leeuwen [1967] p 4). The perspectives within which the problem was discussed owed nothing to the achievements in theological and biblical scholarship of previous decades; in fact, the document was deliberately framed to exclude these achievements. It conceived of 'revelation' simply as information provided by God about himself, and of faith simply as intellectual assent to the propositions in which such information was contained.

This *schema* was debated during the third week of November 1962. Its rejection by a majority of the council fathers, and its subsequent removal from the agenda by Pope John, provided one of the first clear indications that the council was not prepared to be dictated to by the curial theologians. A joint sub-commission, drawn from the Theological Commission and the Secretariat for Christian Unity, was set up to redraft it (cf Rynne [1963] pp 140–173). In the second *schema*, produced by this sub-commission, the first two chapters were entitled: 'The Revealed Word of God' and 'Divine Inspiration and Interpretation of Sacred Scripture' (Tavard [1966] p 4). This draft was approved in commission on 27 March 1963 (cf Dupuy [1968] p 89). It was never debated but, between June 1963 and April 1964, some two hundred and eighty written comments were submitted to the commission. Amongst the features of the draft which, as these written comments showed, were especially appreciated, there are three that are of particular interest to us.

In the first place, revelation is no longer conceived of simply as information provided by God about himself. There is also a hint of the recognition that, if revealed truth is saving truth, it must throw some light upon the human condition. Thus the text says that, by divine revelation, 'the truth about God and about man in Christ shines forth for us.'[2]

In the second place, the draft stressed that the *magisterium* is not superior to the word of God, but serves it. In the third place, the 'gospel', which the Council of Trent had described as 'the source of all saving truth and of all ordering of custom and behaviour',[3] is no longer understood simply as a matter of 'eye-witness accounts', but rather of preaching and proclamation. In spite of these improvements, however, the text remained 'too obviously a compromise' (Van Leeuwen [1967] p 5) between irreconcilable positions.

The mixed sub-commission which had been set up in response to the crisis of November 1962 had proved increasingly unwieldy. On 7 March 1964 it was replaced by a sub-committee of the Theological Commission, which included, for the first time, scholars such as Yves Congar who had been ostentatiously left out at earlier stages. (Unhappily, the drafting committee never included sufficient biblical scholars; a fact which was to leave its mark on the final *Constitution*). The new committee produced a third draft, which 'represented an entirely new approach to the subject' (Baum [1967] p 52). This draft was debated at the third session of the council, during the first week of October 1964 (cf Rynne [1965] pp 35–48). Again, there are three features of this draft which are worth recording.

In the first place, 'revelation' is now understood as 'dialogal' in structure: as a matter of interpersonal communication between God and man. As we shall see, the implications of this shift (not that the council spelt them out, or was even necessarily aware of them) for the theology of doctrinal development, and for our understanding of what we mean by 'dogma', are considerable. In its sharpest form, the contrast between this notion of revelation and that which was contained in the original schema may be expressed in terms of the difference between making a 'declaration of love' to someone, and simply providing him with information. (cf Dupuy [1968] pp 94–95)

In the second place, the discussion of the relationship between scripture and tradition has now become a discussion of the role of scripture as a form of tradition. The focus of concern is no longer: What is in which documents? It is now rather: What are the forms in which the reality of revelation is communicated to us? (ibid p 96) This shift in emphasis, which involved the recovery of a far richer, and in fact more traditional notion of tradition, is evidence of the influence of Père Congar on the work of the commission.

In the third place, this draft is significant for the abandonment of a distinction which had for many years exercised considerable influence in scholastic theology; the distinction between 'remote' and 'proximate' norms of faith. If (for the time being) we take the term *magisterium* to refer to those who exercise teaching office in the church, then there is obviously a trivial sense in which authoritative teaching, authoritative interpretation of scripture, performed today is 'closer' to us than authoritative interpretation at the time of Trent, or in the middle ages, or in the fifth century. In this sense, pronouncements by the contemporary *magisterium* are clearly more 'proximate', less 'remote' declarations of the word of God than other declarations made in earlier ages.

However, in order to see how dangerous the distinction can become, when it is taken to mean that the contemporary *magisterium* is, as it were, 'more important' than the scripture it purports to interpret, we can turn to a little book, written at the height of the modernist crisis, and thoroughly respectable in its time, entitled : *The Living Magisterium and Tradition.* There we read : 'The *magisterium* of the Church is the source, the organ, the criterion of revealed truth. To it all else is referred and from it all else is proved'.[4] Taken at face value, such a position would prevent any appeal to scripture or the history of the church as a basis from which critically to assess the vagaries of current teaching in the church.

We could, however, approach the problem another way, and ask: Is the ordinary catholic, who has neither the time nor the training to engage in scholarly research, entitled to trust, today, the accredited preachers of the gospel in the church, without thereby being accused of being either irrational or superstitious? Surely the answer is: Yes. And, in this sense, *magisterium*, or accredited teaching, will be for him the 'proximate' rule or guide of his belief.

It is one thing, however, to say that, in general, a catholic is entitled to trust the accredited preachers of the gospel as guides to his christian belief and understanding, and is not obliged, before he can hope to hear the gospel, personally to undertake an exhaustive study of scripture, history and theology. It is quite another thing for the holders of apostolic office to say to everybody else (scholars included): Do not dare to appeal to scripture or tradition in order to disagree with whatever we happen to say; our view of things is the 'proximate norm' for your belief.

Because the distinction between 'proximate' and 'remote norms of belief' hopelessly confuses these two quite distinct issues, and has far too often been misunderstood and used in the latter sense, the council performed a considerable service in abandoning it.

As a result of the debate on this third draft, a very similar fourth draft was produced, the first three chapters of which were now given the titles which they were to retain in the final version. One of the more significant additions in this draft, to which we shall return, was the inclusion of the assertion that the *magisterium* has the duty of 'devoutly listening to' the word of God.

Apart from a few detailed textual emendations, which need not concern us, the fourth draft was almost identical with the fifth and final text, adopted by the council on 29 October 1965. Out of two thousand two hundred and forty bishops present, only twenty-three voted against Chapter 1, fifty-five against Chapter 2, and twenty-seven against the text as a whole (cf Rynne [1966] p 239). When the *Dogmatic Constitution* was solemnly promulgated on 18 November 1965, two thousand three hundred and forty-four voted *placet* and only six *non placet* (ibid p 246).

'Whereas in the 1962 session the chief point of controversy seemed to be the Scripture-tradition problem, it had become clear by 1964 that the Scripture-tradition question is merely indicative of a much deeper question, the nature of revelation itself' (Moran [1967] p 33; cf Tavard [1966] p 7). If we regard the council as a sign-post, indicating the direction in which broad currents of thought within the church were turning at that period, then few features of the history of the *Constitution* are more significant than the movement towards a focusing on the problem of revelation itself. The realisation that the problem of scripture and tradition could not be solved in the terms in which it was initially posed was also of considerable importance, as was the movement towards the recognition that the *magisterium* is subordinate to that word of God to which it bears witness, and which it may not claim to 'possess'. In the next three chapters, we shall consider each of these points in turn, in the light of the text of the *Constitution*. Although the *Constitution* only contains one brief statement on the problem of doctrinal development, in the narrow sense, even this brief survey of its history may have indicated why it is that the problems underlying the three-year debate which produced the final text are, nevertheless, precisely those problems with which any study of doctrinal development is bound to concern itself.

NOTES

1. This is the title of chapter 6 in the final version: schema (draft) 1 had 'Holy Scripture in the Church'; schema 2 'The Use of Holy Scripture in the Church'; cf Tavard [1966] pp 3–8.
2. 'Qua revelatione veritas tam de Deo quam de homine in Christo nobis illucescit' (quoted from Dupuy [1968] p 89). Compare this with article 2 of the final text: 'Intima autem per hanc revelationem tam de Deo quam de hominis salute veritas nobis in Christo illucescit'.
3. '[Fons] omnis et salutaris veritatis et morum disciplinae' (Denzinger, 783).
4. 'Ecclesiae magisterium ita est fons, organum, criterium veritatis revelatae ut cetera eo referantur et inde sint probanda' (Bainvel [1905] p 56).

2

REVELATION

'Any theory about the development of dogma rests essentially on the idea of revelation' (Hammans [1967] p 54). In other words, shifts in our understanding of what is meant by 'the word of God' necessarily entail corresponding shifts in our understanding of the way in which that word is heard, and responded to, in the course of christian history. We saw, in the previous chapter, that an increasing preoccupation with the problem of revelation was one of the distinctive features of the history of the constitution *Dei Verbum*. In the present chapter, therefore, we shall examine the opening articles of the *Constitution*, in order to discover the more significant aspects of its treatment of this problem.

> *Article 1:* Hearing the word of God with reverence and proclaiming it confidently, this most sacred Synod takes its direction from these words of St John: 'We announce to you the eternal life which was with the Father, and has appeared to us. What we have seen and have heard we announce to you, in order that you also may have fellowship with us, and that our fellowship may be with the Father, and with his son Jesus Christ' (1 Jn 1: 2–3). Therefore, following in the footsteps of the Councils of Trent and of First Vatican, this present Council wishes to set forth authentic teaching about divine revelation and about how it is handed on, so that by hearing the message of salvation the whole world may believe; by believing, it may hope; and by hoping, it may love.

The first thing that strikes one about this article is its resolutely 'dialogal' character: the ground on which the council feels able 'confidently to proclaim' the word of God is not its formal teaching authority, but its conviction that it is 'reverently hearing' the word which it proclaims.

Secondly, it is clear from the text that, since revelation is a 'declaration of love' (a point made, as we shall see, in the following article), the appropriate response is not mere intellectual assent, but a response as personal as the declaration itself. Moreover, the appropriate response to a declaration of love consists not simply in words, but also in actions: love is the way one lives and behaves, not simply an attitude of mind. Thus the implications of this article, especially of its concluding phrases, for the theology of faith (and therefore for the theology of doctrine, and of doctrinal development) are very far-reaching.

Once revelation is conceived of on the analogy of 'dialogue', or 'declaration and response', a question arises to which we shall frequently have occasion to return: namely, is 'doctrine' to be understood as a constituent simply of the 'response', or also of the 'declaration'? To put the point very briefly, for the time being, if we wish to speak of a 'development' or 'evolution' of doctrine, are we referring to a development of God's word, or of man's response to that word?

Finally, the article claims that Vatican II is 'following in the footsteps of the Councils of Trent and First Vatican'. This phrase, which was added at the request of several council fathers (cf de Lubac [1968] p 167), bears witness to that concern for doctrinal continuity which one would expect from a general council. Yet it remains simply an *assertion*. There is, at least in this article, no attempt to demonstrate that, underlying the manifest discontinuity between this treatment of revelation and that adopted by Trent and Vatican I (a discontinuity sufficiently evident to have provoked the demand for the inclusion of this phrase!), there is a deeper underlying continuity. It is not, in other words, quite clear what path the footsteps have taken.

Article 2: In his goodness and wisdom, God chose to reveal himself and to make known to us the hidden purpose of his will (cf Eph 1:9) by which through Christ, the Word made flesh, man has access to the Father in the Holy Spirit and comes to share in the divine nature (cf Eph 2: 18; 2 Pet 1: 4). Through this revelation, therefore, the invisible God (cf Col 1: 15; 1 Tim 1: 17) out of the abundance of his love speaks to men as friends (cf Ex 33: 11;

Jn 15: 14–15) and lives among them (cf Bar 3: 38), so that
he may invite and take them into fellowship with himself.
This plan of revelation is realized by deeds and words
having an inner unity: the deeds wrought by God in the
history of salvation manifest and confirm the teaching and
realities signified by the words, while the words proclaim
the deeds and clarify the mystery contained in them. By
this revelation then, the deepest truth about God and the
salvation of man is made clear to us in Christ, who is the
Mediator and at the same time the fullness of all revelation.

Here, the dialogue pattern is strengthened: 'out of the abundance of his love', God 'speaks to men as friends'. The statement that 'This plan of revelation is realised by deeds and
words having an inner unity' is somewhat cumbersome, but
nevertheless of considerable importance. It is hardly a defect
of the text that the nature of this 'inner unity' is not rigorously
explored: it is not the function of a council to resolve complex theological problems that are still under discussion.
Positively, however, the assertion that revelation consists, not
merely in words, but also in deeds, shows how far we have
come from a view of revelation consisting simply in the provision of information. 'The Hebrews shared with most of the
ancient Semitic world . . . a belief in the distinct reality of
the spoken word as a dynamic entity. Often this belief
degenerates into magic; but magic is rather a perversion of a
genuine belief in the power of the word . . . Hebrew uses
"word" where we use "thing" or "deed"'. (McKenzie [1966]
p 938). Revelation is thus 'interpreted activity'. That is,
certain events are understood to be a 'word of God' to man.

Each of the three terms in that definition are of equal importance: *God*, certain *events* in human history, the *interpretation* of those events by human minds.

If the events cannot in some sense be described as the
action of God, then they can hardly be described as God's
revelation. Similarly, if the human interpretation cannot in
some sense be ascribed to God then, again, the whole interpreted event or activity can hardly be described as God's
revelation.

Thus it is that any adequate theology of revelation is, at

the same time, a dynamic theology of the Trinity (cf Tavard [1966] p 8; Baum [1967] p 61). As an ancient liturgical antiphon puts it: *Caritas Pater, gratia Filius, communicatio Spiritus Sanctus*. Moreover, on such an account, man's reception of God's word enters into the very definition of revelation itself: 'A revelation is not fully given until it is received' (Butler B. C. [1967] p 34; this is a central theme in Moran [1967]). But, if human experience is a constitutive element in revelation, then we are tempted to ask the question: Are we to conceive of revelation as a matter of man's understanding of himself and of his future, or as coming to him from 'outside'? To put the question in this way, as a matter of mutually exclusive alternatives, is to confuse the issue (see de Lubac [1968] p 170, for his criticism of Bakker [1967] p 11). Many of the debates during the modernist crisis provide striking evidence of this. Nevertheless, it is not easy to take with sufficient seriousness the function of human experience and self-understanding in the process of revelation, while at the same time safeguarding the God-given nature of that revelation. Nor is it a coincidence that the problem here is very similar to that which lies at the heart of christology: When we say that Jesus Christ is truly God and truly man, what do we mean by 'and'?

The article speaks of the 'history of salvation'. This notion has become increasingly popular in recent years in catholic theology and, especially, in catechetics. Ironically, its popularity has been waxing in catholic circles during the very period in which, in protestant theology (which first gave rise to it during the nineteenth century: cf de Lubac [1968] p 184), it has been on the wane. The appearance of the concept in a conciliar constitution is important in so far as it heralds the end of the non-historical, rationalistic mood that was dominant in catholic theology from the eighteenth century until the end of the second world war. Yet it is not without its difficulties, three of which are worth noticing.

In the first place, there is a temptation to use the apparently historical notion of 'salvation history' non-historically. We are situated *within* history. We can only relate to our past and to our future from where we stand today, within the historical process. Whether or not this condemns us to an inevitable relativism in our hearing of and response to God's word is a question to which we shall frequently have to return. But at least it is clear that we cannot stand outside our history, and view it 'panoramically', from some neutral vantage-point.

In the second place, to say that one part of human history, rather than the whole of it, is—in some special sense—the 'history of salvation', is to raise questions as to which part of human history is to be thus described, and on what criteria. This problem becomes particularly acute when we recognise, as we must, that the 'special' history of salvation does not end with the death of Christ, but continues in the time of the church. Is the continuing special history of salvation restricted to the history of the catholic church (as many accounts of doctrinal development seem to assume), or does it include the history of all christian bodies? What is the relationship, so far as the history of salvation is concerned, between the history of christianity and the rest of human history, both secular and religious?

In the third place, if we use the concept of a history of salvation uncritically, is there not a danger of a certain unreality or holy triumphalism? Is not the history of the Jewish people, and of the christian church, at least as obviously a history of disaster, of darkness, of blindness, of unfreedom, as it is a history of liberation (which is, after all, what 'salvation' means)?

In the closing phrases of the article, Christ is described as being himself 'the fullness of revelation'. Not simply his words or deeds, but the person of Christ himself. It is Christ himself who discloses God to us. Revelation is Christ, acknowledged in faith as Christ, as God's irrevocable, eternal word concerning the future of man. To anyone familiar with classical protestant theology during the first half of this century, such a description comes as no surprise. But it does indicate, once again, how far the council had moved from that pre-conciliar scholastic theology which had assumed that revelation consisted in sets of propositions.

Finally, the recognition that it is Christ himself who is the fullness of revelation radically undercuts biblical fundamentalism, and calls in question the possibility of justifying individual doctrines or practices simply by appealing to individual sentences in scripture—even to individual statements of Jesus himself. In the light of christian faith, individual events described in scripture, or individual passages in scripture in general, can only be described as revelatory in so far as they throw light on, or contribute to, our understanding of the mystery of Christ.

Article 4: (we can, for our purposes, omit article 3) Then, after speaking in many places and varied ways through the prophets, God 'last of all in these days has spoken to us by his son' (Heb 1:1–2). For he sent his Son, the eternal Word, who enlightens all men, so that he might dwell among men and tell them the innermost realities about God (cf Jn 1:1–18). Jesus Christ, therefore, the Word made flesh, sent as 'a man to men', 'speaks the words of God' (Jn 3:34), and completes the work of salvation which his Father gave him to do (cf Jn 5:36; 17:4). To see Jesus is to see his Father (Jn 14:9). For this reason Jesus perfected revelation by fulfilling it through his whole work of making himself present and manifesting himself: through his words and deeds, his signs and wonders, but especially through his death and glorious resurrection from the dead and final sending of the Spirit of truth. Moreover, he confirmed with divine testimony what revelation proclaimed: that God is with us to free us from the darkness of sin and death, and to raise us up to life eternal.

The Christian dispensation, therefore, as the new and definitive covenant, will never pass away, and we now await no further new public revelation before the glorious manifestation of our Lord Jesus Christ (cf 1 Tim 6:14; Tit 2:13).

The affirmation that Christ is 'the fullness of revelation' is here more fully developed: 'For this reason . . . Spirit of truth' (and notice the trinitarian structure of this sentence). Where the final text has 'through his whole work of making himself present and manifesting himself' *tota suiipsius presentia ac manifestatione*, the third draft had: 'through his whole person' *tota sua persona*. The phrase was altered at the demand of the minority, who insisted that the 'person' of Christ is a mystery that is revealed, rather than itself constituting the revelation. Quite apart from indicating the methodological gulf which separated the two 'wings' of the council, this is an interesting sidelight on the problem of doctrinal development. The meaning of the term 'person' has changed dramatically since it was introduced into trinitarian and christological discussion in the early centuries. As a result, those who today are nervous of talking about Christ as a 'human person' run the risk of losing just that balance in christology which the early councils were so anxious to maintain. Thus, in the present case, the third draft was christologically much stronger than the final text, which tends to tell only one half of the story. The commission agreed to modify the phrase, but they pointed to the presence of a similar expression in article 5 of the constitution *Lumen Gentium:* 'the kingdom is made manifest in the very person of Christ'.[1]

Several of the bishops at the council were dissatisfied with the statement that 'The Christian dispensation' is 'the new and definitive covenant'. They wanted to see a specific assertion that revelation ended 'with the death of the last apostle' (cf de Lubac [1968] p 232). It is rather important that they did not get their way. Once the idea that revelation consists in the provision of a list of propositions has been abandoned, the clumsy formula of the decree *Lamentabili*, that revelation was 'completed with the apostles'[2] becomes quite unusable. If revelation does not in some sense 'continue', then Christ, who *is* the revelation, cannot be present to us today. At best, we could be in contact with institutions consequent upon, or statements about that revelation.

But the positive concern underlying the clumsy formula retains its validity. The revelation made in Christ (a constituent element of which is its reception in faith, by the gift of the 'sending of the Spirit of truth') is definitive. God will not call in question his last, eschatological word. '[L]e mystère du Christ est fécond, et ne cesse de projeter sa lumière sur les situations toujours changeantes de l'histoire des hommes' (de Lubac [1968] p 235). In later chapters, we shall discuss whether the history of doctrine must, or even can adequately be described as a 'linear' process; as a process of unfolding evolution. Certainly, the council's affirmation of the definitive nature of revelation in Christ entails an affirmation of trust that the faith of christians (their response to God's unchanging word) will, in different situations, be substantially the same. But, although de Lubac himself firmly subscribes to a theory of the 'homogeneous evolution' of doctrine, both the conciliar text, and his gloss on it which we have just quoted, are quite compatible with a more discontinuous, 'episodic' model of doctrinal history.

The revelation made in Christ is definitive, eschatological. The church's task is to actualise that one word, that unchanging gospel—in its life, institutions, liturgy, preaching and doctrine—in the whole range and variety of contexts and circumstances in which men find themselves.

> *Article 5:* 'The obedience of faith' (Rom 16:26; cf 1:5; 2 Cor 10:5–6) must be given to God who reveals, an obedience by which man entrusts his whole self freely to God, offering 'the full submission of intellect and will to God who reveals', and freely assenting to the truth revealed by him. If this faith is to be shown, the grace of God and the interior help of the Holy Spirit must precede and assist, moving the heart and turning it to God, opening the eyes of the mind, and giving 'joy and ease to everyone in assenting to the truth and believing it'. To bring about an ever deeper understanding of revelation, the same Holy Spirit constantly brings faith to completion by his gifts.

It is fashionable nowadays sharply to contrast faith conceived as an intellectual assent to propositions with a view of faith as 'personal adhesion', patterned on the analogy of personal relationships between human beings. But however inadequate the former conception may be, it cannot simply be replaced by the latter. 'Le coeur a ses raisons que la raison ne connait pas'. But he would be a foolish man who allowed his life to be so dictated by his heart that his head was quite unable to assent to any propositions concerning whom he loved and why. If religious belief is not to be quite blind and irrational then, although human relationships may provide the best analogy for it, that very analogy suggests that we must find some place in our account of belief for 'believing that such-and-such is the case'.

It is therefore not unreasonable to see, in the double description of faith in this article ('"The obedience of faith" . . .
by which man entrusts his whole self freely to God'; 'freely
assenting to the truth revealed by him'), evidence of a 'souci
d'équilibre' (de Lubac [1968] p 245; cf p 248). Yet it also
needs to be said that the two accounts are awkwardly related
one to another, and that their juxtaposition bears witness to
the unresolved conflict between the two theologies at the
council (cf Butler B. C. [1967] pp 34–35).

By its reference to the gifts of the Spirit, the council seems
to have in mind 'wisdom', rather than mere intellectual or
scholarly competence, when it speaks of 'an ever deeper
understanding of revelation'. Does this mean that we can only
speak of 'evolution' or 'progress' in the church's reception of
God's saving word in so far as we can also speak of an increase
(individually or corporately) in holiness? This is a question to
which we shall return.

Article 6, which is concerned with the possibility of 'natural
theology', need not detain us. Although it is not uninteresting,
it is 'une sorte d'appendice' (de Lubac [1968] p 263) to the
chapter. It was imported from a preparatory document on
the 'integral preservation of the treasures of faith', and 'No
attempt was made to clarify the connection of this last section
with the concept of revelation as it was set out in the first
sections' (Van Leeuwen [1967] p 7).

NOTES

1. *Regnum manifestatur in ipsa Persona Christi.* In the text, I have
modified the translation: Abbott, too weakly, has 'the kingdom is
clearly visible in the very person of Christ'. On this whole incident,
cf de Lubac [1968], p 222.
2. The proposition condemned in *Lamentabili* reads: 'Revelatio,
objectum fidei catholicae constituens, non fuit cum Apostolis
completa' (Denzinger, 2021).

3

SCRIPTURE AND TRADITION

We have already seen that the problem of the relationship between scripture and tradition was the chief preoccupation of the first draft submitted to the council, and was at the centre of the stormy debate that took place in November 1962. In effect, that first draft invited Vatican II to close a question which had been left open by both Trent and Vatican I, namely: Is the whole of revelation 'in' scripture, or is 'part' of it only contained 'in' tradition? (cf Tavard [1966] p 15).

The council refused to answer the question either way. It refused to affirm either that the whole of revelation is 'contained in' scripture, or that it is 'partly in' scripture and 'partly in' tradition. According to Hans Küng, 'The theological commission, under pressure from the Curial minority, ended by leaving open the question of the relationship between' (Küng [1971] p 63) scripture and tradition. This statement is not incorrect, but it gives the impression that the final text is simply a compromise, arrived at under the pressures of an overriding concern for the unanimity of conciliar decision. However, as one protestant commentator remarked, to have rejected either proposed position in favour of the other would have been an incorrect admission that they constitute authentic alternatives (cf Leuba [1968] p 480).

As the debate matured during the four years of the council, the whole problematic shifted. Not only did the council's understanding of the *relationship* of scripture to tradition deepen, but the notion of tradition, and the understanding of the relationship of both scripture and tradition to the word of God to which they bear witness, underwent a dramatic transformation. For the moment, it is sufficient briefly to indicate the nature of the shift that took place: we shall return to it when discussing the problem of tradition historically, in a later chapter.

If revelation is understood primarily as divine 'teaching',

then 'it is a question of great urgency whether this teaching is entirely contained in Scripture or whether part of the teaching is contained in tradition alone. But if we understand revelation as divine self-disclosure, as Word of God, then it is essentially undivided' (Baum [1967] p 65). But what do we mean by 'tradition'? The *Constitution* does not provide us with a definition, and this is perhaps just as well. Any attempt to do so would have run the risk of refossilising the debate. However, a definition was attempted by the Faith and Order Conference held at Montreal in 1963. In view of the fact that there is a remarkable convergence between this report and the *Constitution* (cf Leuba [1968] p 478), the definition offered by the former may throw some light on the latter.

The report distinguishes between 'Tradition' (the gospel, the *life* of the church, the presence of Christ in history), 'tradition' (the *process* of handing-on, of communicating the gospel message) and 'traditions' (particular customs, institutions, and so on). The concept of tradition which underlies the greater part of chapter two of the *Constitution* corresponds most closely to the first of these three descriptions.

We have already noticed that the third draft of the *Constitution* replaced the discussion of the relationship between scripture and tradition by a discussion of the role of scripture as a form of tradition. 'The meaning of this change is not merely that tradition [chronologically] preceded Scripture but rather that tradition is more comprehensive and in fact includes Scripture' (Van Leeuwen [1967] p 7). Thus, if we compare the *Constitution* with the texts of Trent and Vatican I, we notice that 'tradition is no longer described as the embodiment of the unchangeable but as growth' (loc cit), as life.

In other words, the questions at the heart of the debate no longer focus on the problem of whether or not revelation is 'partly' in scripture and 'partly' in the traditions. The centres of interest are now the relationships that obtain between tradition, scripture, the present belief and activity of the church, and the nature and function of the *magisterium*.

Article 7: In his gracious goodness, God has seen to it that what he had revealed for the salvation of all nations would abide perpetually in its full integrity and be handed on to all generations. Therefore Christ the Lord, in whom the full revelation of the supreme God is brought to completion (cf 2 Cor 1:20; 3:16; 4:6), commissioned the apostles to preach to all men that gospel which is the source of all saving truth and moral teaching, and thus to impart to them divine gifts. This gospel had been promised in former times through the prophets, and Christ himself fulfilled it and promulgated it with his own lips. This commission was faithfully fulfilled by the apostles who, by their oral preaching, by example, and by ordinances, handed on what they had received from the lips of Christ, from living with him, and from what he did, or what they had learned through the prompting of the Holy Spirit. The commission was fulfilled, too, by those apostles and apostolic men who under the inspiration of the same Holy Spirit committed the message of salvation to writing.

But in order to keep the gospel forever whole and alive within the Church, the apostles left bishops as their successors, "handing over their own teaching role" to them. This sacred tradition, therefore, and sacred Scripture of both the Old and the New Testament are like a mirror in which the pilgrim Church on earth looks at God, from whom she has received everything, until she is brought finally to see him as he is, face to face (cf 1 Jn 3:2).

To some extent, this opening article of chapter two is a step backwards. 'The basic insight of Chapter 1, according to which Christ is the revelation not simply in virtue of his teaching but in his own historical person, life, sufferings and resurrection, seems to have receded temporarily into the background, yielding place to the notion of tradition (or transmission) as the handing-on of speculative truth conveyed in words' (Butler B. C. [1967] p 39). However, as Bishop Butler goes on to point out, 'Two attempts are made to escape from this confusion': the references to 'divine gifts' and to 'ordinances' both suggest a more concrete, less theoretical concept of the content of tradition.

Article 8: And so the apostolic preaching, which is expressed in a special way in the inspired books, was to be preserved by a continuous succession of preachers until the end of time. Therefore the apostles, handing on what they themselves had received, warn the faithful to hold fast to the traditions which they have learned either by word of mouth or by letter (cf 2 Th 2:15), and to fight in defence of the faith handed on once and for all (cf Jude 3). Now what was handed on by the apostles includes everything which contributes to the holiness of life, and the increase in faith of the People of God; and so the Church, in her teaching, life, and worship, perpetuates and hands on to all generations all that she herself is, all that she believes.

This tradition which comes from the apostles develops in the Church with the help of the Holy Spirit. For there is a growth in the understanding of the realities and the words which have been handed down. This happens through the contemplation and study made by believers, who treasure these things in their hearts (cf Lk 2:19, 51), through the intimate understanding of spiritual things they experience, and through the preaching of those who have received through episcopal succession the sure gift of truth. For, as the centuries succeed one another, the Church constantly moves forward toward the fullness of divine truth until the words of God reach their complete fulfilment in her.

The words of the holy Fathers witness to the living presence of this tradition, whose wealth is poured into the practice and life of the believing and praying Church. Through the same tradition the Church's full canon of the sacred books is known, and the sacred writings themselves are more profoundly understood and unceasingly made active in her; and thus God, who spoke of old, uninterruptedly converses with the Bride of his beloved Son; and the Holy Spirit, through whom the living voice of the gospel resounds in the Church, and through her, in the world, leads unto all truth those who believe and makes the word of Christ dwell abundantly in them (cf Col 3:16).

According to Bishop Butler, the sentence 'Now what was handed on . . . all that she believes', may be regarded as the 'most important sentence in our chapter' (Butler B. C. [1967] p 39). Indeed, it could even be said that this book is intended to be little more than an extended commentary and reflection on this article. For this reason, the comments which it is appropriate to make in this chapter can be brief.

Christ, who *is* the revelation, is permanently present in the life, institutions and belief of the church. The whole process of living tradition provides the context in which Christ, God's last word, is encountered in human history. This summary description of the perspective within which the council invites us to reflect on the problem of tradition raises two questions of fundamental importance, to which we shall return in the next chapter.

In the first place, how do we understand this process in which Christ continues to meet his people, in which God's word continues to be heard? Theories of 'doctrinal development', in all their variety, represent one way of attempting to answer this question.

In the second place, what do we understand to be the role of the *magisterium* in this process, and what is the relationship between the function of the *magisterium* and that unique, unrepeatable, privileged witness to Christ which is the new testament?

Article 9: Hence there exist a close connection and communication between sacred tradition and sacred Scripture. For both of them, flowing from the same divine wellspring, in a certain way merge into a unity and tend toward the same end. For sacred Scripture is the word of God inasmuch as it is consigned to writing under the inspiration of the divine Spirit. To the successors of the apostles, sacred tradition hands on in its full purity God's word, which was entrusted to the apostles by Christ the Lord and the Holy Spirit. Thus, led by the light of the Spirit of truth, these successors can in their preaching preserve this word of God faithfully, explain it, and make it more widely known. Consequently, it is not from sacred Scripture alone that the Church draws her certainty about everything which has been revealed. Therefore both sacred tradition and sacred scripture are to be accepted and venerated with the same sense of devotion and reverence.

The concern to hold together the concepts of revelation,

scripture and tradition, in a coherent unity, which characterises this whole chapter of the *Constitution*, is especially evident in this and the following article. It is, however, important to recognise that such a concern does not, of itself, solve the more basic problems at issue. 'While the phrase "the word of God" rightly embraces a subtly complex set of referents, its use at times obscures rather than clarifies the intent of the *Constitution*. At least ten various referents of this phrase may be found (in art 1, 2, 3, 8, 10, 13, 14, 17, 21, 26). The advantages of utilizing the multiplicity of connotations are obvious, since this one category unifies the four major categories (revelation, Scripture, tradition, magisterium). Of each, one can say truly in appropriate contexts that it *is* the word of God. Of each, one can say that it *contains* and that it *imparts* the word. But in doing this it is all too easy to throw a semantic smoke-screen over the critical issues because of a laudable desire to relate God's speech to all these human channels of transmission' (Minear [1966] p 86).

This article is one of those which underwent last-minute modification, on the orders of the pope, in an attempt to satisfy the demands of the conciliar minority. At first sight, the addition of the phrase, 'it is not from sacred Scripture alone that the Church draws her certainty about everything which has been revealed' appears to be a clear victory for the minority, closing doors which the council had taken great pains to keep open (on the history of the addition of this clause, see Caprile [1968] pp 669–677). However, if we put the stress where it belongs, on the term 'certainty', then it is clear that the phrase simply represents a recognition of the role of the church in interpreting scripture. As such, it has proved acceptable to a number of protestant scholars, including Karl Barth himself (cf Barth [1968] p 518; Leuba [1968] p 482; Thurian [1968b] pp 44–45). 'It is unfortunate that the constitution uses the Protestant watchword *sola scriptura* in this negative context, but it was not easy to find an acceptable formula which would avoid it. However, the Doctrinal Commission avoided the phrase *ex sola scriptura* and chose instead *per solam scripturam*; in this way it avoided the impression that it was considering scripture as a defective *source*' (Butler B. C. [1967] p 43).

The last sentence of this article raises a number of interesting questions. After trying out various formulations, the council eventually settled for repeating a famous phrase used by the Council of Trent, and originating from St Basil (cf Congar [1966] p 47). Clearly, its presence in the *Constitution* is due largely to the council's concern for doctrinal continuity. But what *kind* of continuity is thereby achieved or affirmed? Given the vast differences in cultural and linguistic context, and in theological method and concern, how would one show that the mere fact that the same *words* were used in the fourth century by St Basil, in the sixteenth century by Trent, and in the twentieth by Vatican II, establishes that there has been a significant continuity of *meaning*? Must we not say that the council's decision to employ this phrase is evidence of no more than its concern for continuity; that it in no way demonstrates that this continuity has, in any very significant sense, in fact been achieved?

4

DEVELOPMENT AND MAGISTERIUM

The last three chapters have indicated why it is that the opening articles of the constitution *Dei Verbum* provide a convenient framework within which to initiate a discussion of doctrinal change and continuity. Some of the problems come more sharply into focus when we put to the text of articles 8 and 10 the two questions which were raised in the previous chapter. Firstly, how do we understand the process of tradition in which God's word continues to be heard? Secondly, what do we understand to be the role of the *magisterium* in this process?

There have been, in western theology, two broadly distinct ways of conceiving the church's relationship to the God whose Spirit enlivens it, enabling it, in the Spirit, faithfully to hear his word and sacramentally to embody it (cf *Constitution on the Church* 1).

On the one hand, it is possible to stress the Spirit's unfailing guidance of the historical process, keeping the church continually alive and at least minimally faithful to the word that calls it into existence. Here the emphasis will be in the faithfulness of God to his promise, on continuity and maintained identity. This approach has generally characterised catholic theology. It is, therefore, not surprising that article 8, with its emphasis on 'a continuous succession of preachers', and on the fact that the church 'constantly moves forward toward the fullness of divine truth', should represent this 'horizontal' model of the church's relationship to the word and Spirit of God.

On the other hand, if our starting-point is the recognition of the sovereign freedom of God, the emphasis is likely to be on the unpredictability of the patterns of christian history. 'Such is the history of society', said Newman, 'it begins in the poet, and ends in the policeman' (H.S. III p 77). Christianity, in its doctrines, rites and institutions, is not immune from this entropic tendency. But, trusting the grace of God, it will not be surprised when that grace breaks in to chastise, forgive, re-create and make anew. If the first approach looks to the factors making for continuity in christian history, the second (which has been more characteristic of protestant than of catholic theology), with its emphasis on the 'vertical' action of God in history, is less perplexed by the discontinuities that are also discernible in that history.

In broad outline, however, both catholic and protestant theologies[1] agree on the importance of the process of living tradition, as the context within which Christ, the revelation of God, is made present to men in every age. To put it another way, all are agreed that Christ 'is present . . . when the Holy Scriptures are read in the church' (*Constitution on the Liturgy* 7).

Moreover, the last sentence of the first paragraph of article 8, taken together with article 12 of the *Constitution on the Church*, show the extent to which catholic theology currently stresses that it is the *whole* church which is the bearer of the tradition (or, in scholastic language, the 'subject of infallibility'). In this second chapter of *Dei Verbum*, 'there is nothing now left of an identification of tradition with the magisterium' (Van Leeuwen [1967] p 8).

According to the second paragraph of article 8, however, 'as the centuries succeed one another, the Church constantly moves forward toward the fullness of divine truth'. It is when the church's confidence in the abiding presence of Christ in his Spirit is expressed in this manner that sharp divergences begin to appear. (We shall have occasion, in a later chapter, to test the accuracy of Bishop Butler's assertion that this paragraph of article 8 'is practically a précis of Newman's theory of the development of doctrine'—Butler, B. C. [1967] p 40).

According to the *Constitution*, the successive actualisation of revelation which constitutes the process of tradition represents a *progress* in the church's hearing of the word of God (cf Leuba [1968] p 490). It is at this point that most protestant theologians (most, not all; cf Thurian [1968a] p 73), and increasing numbers of catholics, become uneasy. Leuba points out that, while the Montreal report speaks of this successive actualisation, it never considers it as progress (cf Leuba [1968] p 491). 'Doctrinal development is not a matter of continuous and cumulative growth or explicitation of the Church's knowledge of revelation or (even worse from the Protestant's point of view) of the Church's self-awareness or self-understanding' (Lindbeck [1967] p 66).

It would be foolish to criticise the *Constitution* for embracing, in this article, an 'evolutionary' or 'progressive' view of doctrinal history. In view of the suspicion with which 'official' catholic thinking has traditionally regarded all talk of doctrinal 'change' or 'development', it was something of an achievement for this paragraph to have been included at all. Moreover, even as recently as a decade ago, most catholics writing on the subject assumed that some such 'evolutionary' or 'progressive' view of doctrinal history was justified. Nevertheless, as Congar has pointed out, commenting on this article, it represents the recognition by Vatican II (unlike Vatican I) of 'the problem of the evolution or development of dogma', but 'at a time when it had already been reformulated in the thinking of informed theologians' (Congar [1970a] p 87). Built-in obsolescence is today the fate, not only of cars but also of constitutions. Again and again, we shall have to return to the question: Is a 'linear', 'cumulative', 'progressive' view of doctrinal history demanded by the claims of christian belief, and justified by history?

To conclude these remarks on article 8, we can notice one difficulty which any 'linear' model of doctrinal development immediately runs up against: 'comment concilier la continuité de l'histoire de l'Eglise et des dogmes avec la possibilité de se ressourcer dans les origines?' (Leuba [1968] p 492). Gregory Baum is, I think, correct in saying that, if we take seriously that concept of revelation which is dominant in the *Constitution*, then it follows that 'dogma is relative, ie relative to divine revelation' (Baum [1967] p 63). But until we have answered Leuba's question, what critical principles have we with which to ensure that this relativity, or subordination of dogma to revelation, is effectively maintained? Baum is aware of the fact that the *Constitution* does not come to grips with this problem. Tavard, unfortunately, evades the problem by uncritically assuming the propriety of the 'evolutionary' or 'progressive' tone of the *Constitution's* treatment (cf Tavard [1966] p 24).

Article 10: Sacred tradition and sacred Scripture form one sacred deposit of the word of God, which is committed to the Church. Holding fast to this deposit, the entire holy people united with their shepherds remain always steadfast in the teaching of the apostles, in the common life, in the breaking of the bread, and in prayers (cf Acts 2:42), so that in holding to, practising, and professing the heritage of the faith, there results on the part of the bishops and faithful a remarkable common effort.

The task of authentically interpreting the word of God, whether written or handed on, has been entrusted exclusively to the living teaching office of the Church, whose authority is exercised in the name of Jesus Christ. This teaching office is not above the word of God, but serves it, teaching only what has been handed on, listening to it devoutly, guarding it scrupulously, and explaining it faithfully by divine commission and with the help of the Holy Spirit; it draws from this one deposit of faith everything which it presents for belief as divinely revealed.

It is clear, therefore, that sacred tradition, sacred Scripture, and the teaching authority of the Church, in accord with God's most wise design, are so linked and joined together that one cannot stand without the others, and that all together and each in its own way under the action of the one Holy Spirit contribute effectively to the salvation of souls.

The statement that 'This teaching office [*magisterium*] is not above . . . divinely revealed' clearly subordinates church teaching to divine revelation. The same emphasis reappears later in the *Constitution*, in article 21: 'Therefore, like the Christian religion itself, all the preaching of the Church must be nourished and ruled by sacred Scripture'. The third draft had expressed this more strongly: 'all the Church's preaching must always look to Scripture as norm and authority by which it is ruled and judged' (quoted from Baum [1967] p 69; cf Dupuy [1968] pp 116–117). From the point of view of the theology of the *magisterium*, one of the most important changes introduced into the fourth draft was the addition of the phrase *'pie audit'* ('listening to it devoutly'). Dupuy's comment on this addition is, however, a trifle over-optimistic: 'toute la théologie du magistère est rééquilibrée par ces deux mots' (Dupuy [1968] p 114).

The importance of this article consists in the extent to which it provides evidence of the council's determination to put an end to a state of affairs in which, in practice, papal teaching and even curial directives had come to be regarded as more or less immune from critical evaluation by biblical scholars, historians, theologians and the common sense of the believing community. Nevertheless, while gratefully acknow-ledging the council's intention, it is important not to exag-gerate the extent of its achievement.

Hans Küng, commenting on the final paragraph of the article, is quite correct when he says that 'Vatican II suffered from first to last from the fact that the question of what really is the ultimate, supreme norm for the renewal of the Church was left undecided' (Küng [1971] p 63). Vatican II did not, nor (if we are to be realistic) could it have been expected to, convincingly grasp that nettle. However, Küng's confidence that there is, and that there can be shown to be, a *single* 'supreme norm' may be unfounded. A naive biblicism would be a poor alternative to a naive authoritarianism as the criterion by which the christian search for truth is to be assessed.

The grammar of the article is often ambiguous: 'Le Magis-tère enseigne-t-il la vérité parce qu'il en possède le mandat, ou possède-t-il ce mandat dans la mesure où il enseigne la vérité?' (Leuba [1968] p 494). It is easy to say that the func-tion of the *magisterium* is, first and foremost, devoutly to listen to the word of God. But what are the appropriate means it should take in order to do so? Simplifying them in order to highlight the problem, there would seem to be at least three different ways in which this 'listening' might be understood.

In the first place, it could be suggested that the holders of apostolic office should simply 'listen to', and learn from, biblical scholars and theologians, since such scholars are presumably professionally equipped to 'hear' the word, in its scriptural expression, with accuracy. However, while magisterial teaching which ignores the findings of critical scholarship remains a scandal, the suggestion that responsibility or church teaching should be handed over to academics might well turn out, on examination, to rest on one form of that intellectualist, theoretical conception of revelation against which the council was rightly reacting.

In the second place, it could be suggested that the holders of apostolic office should simply 'listen to', and learn from, the christian community as a whole. It is, after all, in the church as a whole that the Spirit lives, and christian experience is undoubtedly a privileged source for theological reflection. Yet today, as at all times, the christian community is animated, not only by the spirit of the Gospel, but also by less desirable forces. If church teaching were simply to reflect the present mind of the majority of church members, for example, are there adequate guarantees that, in so doing, it would be faithfully responding to the disturbing, unfashionable authority of the word of God, the Lord of the church?

In the third place, if the Spirit at all times effectively guides and illuminates church leaders in the exercise of their office, then they may at all times be presumed to have listened devoutly to God's word. Therefore, it could be argued, 'devout listening' today consists in resolutely refusing to depart from the judgements expressed by one's predecessors. It is not implausible to suggest that the promulgation of *Humanae Vitae*, and the neglect by Paul vi of the advice given to him by the commission which he himself had set up, was at least partially a consequence of just such an understanding of what it meant for him devoutly to listen to the word of God.

Three unsatisfactory alternatives. Later, we may be able to throw a little more light on the problem. But, for all its emphasis on the subordination of church teaching to revelation, the *Constitution* will be of little help to us.

There is another, closely related ambiguity in the phrasing of the article; an ambiguity which, we as shall see, frequently characterises theological assertions. Is this article a description of how in fact the *magisterium* functions, and has functioned in history? Or is it a recommendation as to the way in which the *magisterium* ought to act? Or is it both and, if so, what is the relationship between the descriptive and prescriptive claims? Such questions take us into the heart of an exceedingly complex set of problems concerning the sense, or senses, in which doctrinal statements may be said to be true or false. Any study of the principles of doctrinal development must include some attempt to come to grips with these problems.

The first two chapters of the *Constitution* represent a remarkable deepening and recovery of balance in official catholic teaching on revelation and its transmission. Karl Barth's final verdict on the *Constitution* is significant: 'si jamais il y a eu un concile de réforme, c'était bien celui-là' (Barth [1968] p 522). But this is an acknowledgement of the soundness of the direction in which the *Constitution* points. It would be complacent folly to deny that much hard work remains to be done, and done quickly. Developments during the period since the council ended have highlighted the weaknesses, as well as the strengths, in its achievement.

We have briefly noticed the way in which *Dei Verbum* handled the fundamental themes of revelation, tradition, scripture and the *magisterium*. In the next section, we shall explore these same themes from a different angle. Our starting point will be a sketch of the history of such concepts as 'tradition', 'dogma' and '*magisterium*'.

NOTE

1. When the phrases 'catholic theology' and 'protestant theology' occur, they refer, very generally, to culturally inherited differences in method or preoccupation. It is not my intention to suggest that there is, today, any single characteristically 'catholic' or characteristically 'protestant' theology (cf Lindbeck [1968]). Still less is it my intention to suggest that such differences (often profound) as exist, necessarily constitute divisions in *faith*. Discussion of the limits of theological and doctrinal pluralism lies outside the scope of this chapter.

PART TWO

TRADITION, DOGMA AND
MAGISTERIUM

5

TRADITION AND TRADITIONS

There is an endemic tendency in catholic theology to underestimate the changes and discontinuities in doctrinal history
by assuming that, if a particular term has been in use for a
long time, the succession of historical realities to which it
refers were fundamentally similar. Nobody believes that Peter
the fisherman wore the triple crown or was carried on the
sedia gestatoria through the streets of Antioch, but it is not
always regarded as equally obvious that to refer to him as 'the
first pope' may be rather more misleading than illuminating.
And what, say, of Gregory the Great, or Paul IV or Benedict
XIV? The more conscious we are of the fact that the papacy,
considered as a social, historical phenomenon, has undergone
frequent and dramatic changes in the course of its history, the
less likely we shall be to assume that a phrase such as 'the
meaning of the papacy' refers to some timeless concept un-
affected by linguistic or cultural change.

My concern, in the chapters which follow, is not so much
with the history of individual doctrines, but rather with the
history of some aspects of the conceptual frameworks within
which individual doctrines have been affirmed and understood. This is not to deny that the history of the concept of
'tradition' (with which the present chapter is concerned) is
the history of a concept the meaning of which includes a
strictly theological component. It is simply to draw attention
to the fact that the way in which we understand such 'formal'
concepts as 'tradition' and 'dogma' affects the way in which
we view each and every article of christian belief. It affects
our approach to the whole problem of continuity and discontinuity in christian life, belief and understanding.

It is reasonable to expect that we shall find, in the history of
any concept which has been a feature of christian discourse
for many centuries, an element of progressive clarification
and differentiation. Questions are not answered until they are

asked. And, once asked, they stay on the agenda. Even if they
get forgotten, they continue to affect the subsequent history
of the concept because, when they *were* asked, they deflected
debate and reflection in one direction rather than another.
Thus there is an element of unidirectionality or irreversibility
in the history of ideas (and this may turn out to be relevant
to the problem of the 'irreformability' of dogmatic statements).

But we may also find that such concepts have undergone a
degree of impoverishment, or restriction, or dramatic change
of meaning, in the course of their history. If so, this will be
important when we come to ask in what sense the total process can adequately be described as one of doctrinal 'development'.

'Tradition', in current English usage, is what the Americans
love about the English. If someone says, 'I think your traditions are wonderful', the chances are that he is referring to the
State Opening of Parliament, to the complex gastronomic
rituals of a Cambridge college, or to Stratford-on-Avon. There
is an element of affectionate interest in a decorative but
fundamentally useless past.

The term 'dogma' usually refers to something stated in such
a manner as to inhibit rational discussion ('he's very dogmatic'). The implication often is that, if the claim were to be
dispassionately examined, it would turn out to be un-
warranted. There is, in other words, in our everyday use of
the term, an implied element of irrationality and obscurantism.

My reason for drawing attention to these overtones is that
they inevitably influence our attitude towards the terms in
question. It is not possible to do theology in a psychological
vacuum. But the particular colouring such terms have acquired may do less damage if we make it explicit from the
start.

In order to find our way back to the beginnings of the
history of the concept of tradition in christian thought, it may
be useful to pause for a moment in the eighteenth century.
The enlightenment set in opposition opinions received on
other people's authority and opinions formed by the exercise
of one's own reason. 'It set up a rationalist individualism that
asked people to prove their assumptions or else regard them as

arbitrary. In effect it set out to destroy not only the religious tradition but all tradition.' (Lonergan [1972b] p 110).

To make the point less polemically, the eighteenth century saw the emergence of two sharply differentiated epistemological styles. On the one hand, there were those whose contention that it was intellectually disreputable to rely on received opinions was partly due to the realisation that these opinions were formed in a different situation, in the context of different problems. Thus an emergent scientific consciousness tended to regard 'traditionalism' as more or less identical with obscurantism.

On the other hand, there were those who suspected that reliance on one's own unaided judgement, and a suspicion of inherited wisdom, was a dangerous and illusory form of intellectual pride. Similarly, there was a fear of the tendency to disengagement, to lack of 'commitment', on the part of the man who must have proved everything for himself before he will take the risk of entering upon a course of action. 'Rationalism', in so far as it became a term of abuse in theological circles, carried both these overtones, as is clear, for example, from Newman's *University Sermon* on 'Faith and Reason, Contrasted as Habits of Mind' (U.S. pp 176–201).

But, although the overtones of this debate still survive in the popular usage of the term 'tradition', and although, like the poor, both mentalities are always with us, we are in a position to appreciate that the opposition between them is not as absolute as it once seemed. For one thing, it is possible that distinct epistemological styles are desirable in different areas of human inquiry. The pattern of discovery in the natural sciences, for example, may be governed by a different cognitive interest from that which operates in the search for historical understanding (cf Habermas [1972] pp 301–317).

In order to unpack that suggestion a little, let us go back to the distinction which we noticed in the Montreal report, (p 20 above) between tradition as 'process' and as 'content'. Each of us is the product of the process of tradition. Our opinions and attitudes, beliefs and expectations, are in large measure formed and influenced by the past which we have inherited.[1] We may slowly come to that maturity which enables a man to assess and evaluate the content of the historical process, the traditioning-process, in which he lives. But our concrete involvement in the process of tradition precedes our ability creatively to evaluate it. We never stand outside that process. We have no option as to whether or not we shall be involved in it, or relate to it. We *do* have an option as to whether we relate to it negatively—either by uncritical rejection, or by letting ourselves simply be carried along in the flow of custom and popular opinion; or positively—by attempting creatively to be faithful to the insights, events and achievements of the past by critically evaluating them, and by attempting to *re-read* the past in the light of our present situation and future needs.

By a somewhat indirect route, we have now arrived rather near to the biblical concept of tradition. In the time of the old testament, the 'earlier experience gave meaning to the later event, which in turn threw light on the earlier experience' (Congar [1966] p 3; cf pp 18, 22). (Consider, for example, the successive 're-readings' which the event of the exodus underwent during these centuries.) Theologically, the justification for this continual re-reading of the past in the light of the present, or *midrash*,[2] was the conviction that there was a God-given unity of meaning and purpose in history, and that the God who provoked the earlier events was, in the unchanging fidelity of his covenant-love, holding out the same promise, and inviting the same response in the present.

So in the old testament the process of tradition is the life of the whole people. The content of the tradition is God's declaration of life and love, his promise of salvation, mediated through the forms of the people's response: both the positive forms of a life of faith and obedience, and the negative forms of infidelity.

The contexts in which old testament traditions (in the sense of particular aspects of the content of tradition) were mediated were, above all, the family and the cult. Within the family, the message was 'traditioned', the inherited wisdom of the people was communicated from generation to generation. In the cult, the great events of the past, which gave to the people their understanding of their identity and their mission, were actualised and relived, re-read and interpreted.

The elements which mediated the message included, from an early period, 'certain confessional formulas' (cf Lengsfeld [1969] p 34). In a society in which oral tradition was a principal means of historical communication, short sayings—especially expressions of memory, praise, faith and trust—played a particularly important role.

This structure survived in the early christian communities. The process of tradition is still understood to be the ongoing life of the whole community, and the content of tradition is still God's saving message. The fact that the message had now taken on a new dimension of finality, because of the eschatological nature of Christ's death and resurrection, did not affect the structure of the concept of tradition. Similarly, the privileged contexts for the transmission of the tradition are still the life of the family, the local community and, in particular, its worship. Finally, there was still the tendency to articulate the message of life in brief confessional formulas (we shall return to this in the next chapter).[3]

For the first three centuries of the christian era, the extent to which the whole life of the church is seen as the bearer of the tradition 'is affirmed so emphatically that it can only be translated into images taken from the biological order' (Congar [1966] pp 24-25). Thus the custom of using organic analogies to express the church's understanding of the process of tradition dates from very early in christian history. During this period, the term 'tradition' (*paradosis*) comes increasingly to be used of the content rather than the process—but this is no more than a shift of emphasis.

From the early middle ages until the end of the thirteenth century, tradition continues to be understood as the whole process of the church's historical life, and the content of that process is expressed in the entire range of christian customs, beliefs and worship and, above all, in the bible in which it received its initial and privileged embodiment. In such a situation, particular elements in the total reality are not clearly distinguished one from another, from the point of view of their normative character. Therefore, in view of the strong sense that what is contained in the process and expressed in the content is the reality of God's self-communication in Christ; in view, that is, of the strong sense that the whole life

of the church is life 'in the Spirit', it is hardly surprising that
terms such as 'scripture', revelation', 'inspiration', refer to a
broad range of christian writings and activities (cf Congar
[1966] p 92; Tavard [1959] p 15).

In other words, before events caused the emergence of
normative criteriological questions the particular components of the total reality—bible, bishops, theologians, faithful—
are not seen as rival 'authorities', but rather as complemen-
tary constituents of one complex whole: the process whereby
the apostolic tradition is sustained and enlightened by the
Spirit of the risen Christ. This large generalisation is not
intended to be an invitation to look at the early medieval
situation through rose-tinted spectacles. An undifferentiated
consciousness is also an uncritical consciousness. As Congar
says, 'Medieval writers had no difficulty in finding everything in Scripture, since their principles of exegesis provided
them with the necessary means' (Congar [1966] p 113).

Commenting on the early centuries, Congar notes that
'tradition involves not merely a recollection, but also a
deepening of insight . . . it involves not merely a fidelity
of memory, but also a fidelity of living, vital adherence' (p 15).
This rich concept of christian 'memory' would survive as long
as the biblical concept of faith as personal response to the
living God remained effectively alive in christian thought. It
is a concept which is currently returning to the centre of
interest in catholic theology, as we learn to overcome the
rationalism of recent centuries.

It is important to notice that, throughout the middle ages,
there was no question of any consciousness of dogmatic
development in the modern sense. Thus the fifth century
Commonitorium of Vincent of Lerins, which will be quoted by
almost all participants in the reformation debates, was virtually ignored for a thousand years (cf Rahner [1969b] p 207).
Walgrave's assertion that the fathers, although unaware of the
problem of doctrinal development, had an 'existential awareness' of the 'fact of development' which 'may have been more
lively than that of a contemporary scholar who has objectified
it as a problem to solve' (Walgrave [1972] p 83), is possibly
misleading and certainly difficult to verify. He is on surer
ground when he straightforwardly admits that 'St Thomas—

and, one may add, St Bonaventure—did not have to face the problem of development and were unaware of it' (p 100). Medieval theologians certainly knew of what we would now call 'theological' development, growth in theological understanding, but the concept of progress in the 'deposit of faith' itself was unknown to them.

The Gregorian reforms of the twelfth century, involving a markedly increased emphasis on papal authority, may have been primarily an expression of political needs and concerns, but their theological consequences were considerable. Congar describes the shift in perspective that took place as a 'transition from an appreciation of the ever active *presence of God* to that of *juridical powers* put at the disposal of, and perhaps even handed over as its property to, "the Church", ie the hierarchy' (Congar [1966] p 135; cf Congar [1970b] pp 152–153).

For our purpose, there are two aspects of this shift which are of particular importance. In the first place, during this period, there took place a shrinkage in the notion of the church. Increasingly, the term came to refer, no longer to the whole community, but only to the clergy. There was, at the same time, a similar shrinkage in the opposite direction, as sectarian groups emerged, identifying themselves as the 'true church'. Theologically, there is perhaps little to choose between these two forms of sectarianism.

In the second place, the concept of ecclesiastical authority as that of the exercise of a ministry through whose activity God is present to his people was gradually supplanted by a concept of personally possessed power and authority, bestowing rights and privileges, rather than responsibilities. This is the period in which bishops, including the pope, begin to be spoken of as 'vicars of Christ', as if Christ, the revelation of God, were absent from the life of his people. It is hardly surprising that the increasingly grandiose political claims made for the papacy by the medieval canonists should have provoked reaction and, eventually, explosion.

Towards the end of the thirteenth century, Henry of Ghent asked a fateful question: '"Must we rather believe the authorities of this doctrine [Sacred Scripture] than those of the Church, or the other way round?"' (Quoted Tavard

[1959] p 23). Once that question was asked, there was no going back. Soon, everybody was asking it, and the split between scripture and church authority, and therefore between scripture and tradition, had taken place.

We have seen that, for a long period, there was a tendency to lump together all aspects of the church's life and practice as constituting the content of tradition. It was inevitable that, sooner or later, the question should emerge: are *all* church customs and 'traditions' equally sound, equally authoritative for christian thought and activity, merely because they have been inherited from the past? Is it not possible to appeal to scripture against certain customs and beliefs, even ancient ones? The tragedy of the late-medieval context is not that such questions should have arisen, but that they should have been expressed in a form, and in a climate of debate, which rendered impossible their adequate solution.

Once the appeal to scripture is cast in the form of an appeal to the authority of God, the 'author' (*auctor*) of scripture, over against the 'merely human' claims made by canon lawyers on behalf of ecclesiastical and political authority, then it is a matter of 'choice between submission to God and submission to human bidding. Put in this way, the issue was never in doubt' (Congar [1966] p 142). The emergence, in an unacceptable sense, of the battle-cry of *scriptura sola*, became inevitable. Almost equally inevitable was a reaction in terms of 'the church alone' or 'tradition alone'.

The decree on tradition, promulgated by the Council of Trent on 8 April 1546, so dominated modern catholic theology for many years that the complex and flexible earlier uses of the concept of tradition were unknown or ignored. Unfortunately, moreover, the tridentine decree was regularly misinterpreted by being read through post-tridentine spectacles. 'The concern of the Council was not primarily to determine the relations between Scripture and Tradition, nor between Scripture and "the traditions": it was to defend the Catholic positions attacked by the Reformers.' (Bévenot [1963] p 333). In the light of the modern debates on the 'sources of revelation', it is important to notice that *traditiones* at Trent 'should be rendered "observances"', and does not refer to tradition as a source of revelation' (Murray [1967] p 53; cf Bévenot

[1963], Ratzinger [1966]). When 'the Fathers' of Trent were discussing *"traditiones"*, they had in mind neither Tradition in its modern sense, nor *Paradosis* in the sense current in the early Church, but the traditional observances of the Church of their day . . . in their discussions *oral* tradition is scarcely mentioned, if at all' (Bévenot [1963] pp 334–335). Moreover, the *traditiones* with which they were primarily concerned were those christian observances believed to be apostolic and, as such, of binding authority.

It is important to be clear about what Trent was, and was not, discussing. It is also important to notice how impoverished the concept of tradition has become. At Trent, the word is almost always used in the plural (in marked contrast to Vatican II), and refers to only one small aspect of that total reality to which I previously referred as 'tradition as content'. The decree refers not at all to tradition as the whole process of the historical life of the church.[4]

It is by now a commonplace that the decree of Trent did not commit catholic theology to the view that revelation was 'partly' contained in scripture and 'partly' in the *traditiones*. Geiselmann's pioneer work on this problem placed catholic scholarship permanently in his debt (Geiselmann [1962]). Nevertheless, the significance he attached to the replacement, during the council, of *'partim . . . partim'* by *'et . . . et'*, was excessive. 'One has only to remember what happens when a committee draws up a statement for publication . . . One can imagine one of the drafters saying: "So-and-so objected to *partim*", and another saying: "All right, we can drop it; it doesn't affect the main issue"' (Bévenot [1963] p 344).

More seriously, the concentration on the problem of the 'material sufficiency' of scripture in the debate which followed the publication of Geiselmann's early studies 'resulted in undue narrowing of the inquiry . . . [it obscured] the real background to the Tridentine decree' (Ratzinger [1966] p 50). This was partly due to the fact that 'Geiselmann . . . perhaps remained within the general framework of the controversy in which the relations between Scripture and Tradition are viewed only from the quantitative angle, as it were, of material content' (Congar [1966] p 377). In other words, his work suffered because of a tendency to assume as adequate the impoverished conception of revelation which characterised much of the catholic theology of the period.

We shall be concerned, in a later chapter, with the history of the concept of *magisterium*. But it is worth noticing, in passing, that Trent did not even use the word. However, just as the medieval debates had shifted the emphasis in the notion of tradition from 'tradition as process' to 'tradition as content' or 'deposit', so the centuries after Trent saw a shift from the notion of tradition as 'deposit' to tradition seen 'from the viewpoint of the transmitting organism' (ibid p 182). Since the theology of the church was reduced to a theology of church structures, with the hierarchy as the focus of attention, it is not surprising that the 'transmitting organism' should come to be seen, not as the church as a whole, but as the ecclesiastical hierarchy. This tendency hardened, in mainstream catholic theology, during the nineteenth century, with the distinction between 'active tradition' (the hierarchy in action), and 'objective tradition' (what the hierarchy transmitted). Thus Mackey, whose study of *The Modern Theology of Tradition* covers the period from the middle of the nineteenth to the middle of the twentieth century, can say that 'the principal line of thought in the period under review amounts to the identification of tradition with magisterium' (Mackey [1962] p 1).

The social and cultural revolution of the renaissance, together with the excessive claims made for ecclesiastical authority by the medieval canonists, rendered more or less inevitable the explosive reformation debates concerning tradition and authority.

The social and cultural revolutions of the nineteenth century, together with the excessive claims made for ecclesiastical authority by theologians operating within a primarily juridical conceptual framework, made another, similar debate similarly inevitable. Whether we regard this new explosion as having taken place during the modernist crisis, or whether we regard that crisis as merely the prelude to the even more interesting state of affairs in the church today, is a question which—at this stage—can be left undecided. My purpose, in offering this rapid sketch of the history of the concept of tradition, has simply been to provide the materials

for theological reflection on the significance of that history for
the problem of doctrinal development.

NOTES

1. Cf the illustration of the engineer who trusts his slide-rule in
Lonergan [1972a] pp 46–47.
2. 'In modern exegesis *midrash* designates a type of writing based
on a distinctive Jewish use of the OT; here *use* is a better word than
interpretation' (McKenzie [1966], p 574).
3. It will become clear how heavily dependent this chapter is on
Congar [1966]. Hanson assumes, unjustifiably, that Congar's aim
is 'to squeeze a little more revelation out of the Bible than would
be there without squeezing' (Hanson [1962] p 242). Hanson is
considerably less sensitive to problems of hermeneutic than Congar. Moreover, according to Bévenot, in Hanson's 'exasperating
book . . . patristic texts [are] mistranslated or misdirected
against what is, to a great extent, a caricature of the Roman
Catholic position' (Bévenot [1963] p 346).
4. That judgement hardly needs qualifying even if Ratzinger is
correct in suggesting that Cervini's speech of 28 February 1546,
appealing to a concept of tradition significantly wider than simply
'observances', left its mark on the final decree: cf Ratzinger
[1966].

CREED AND DOGMA

We saw, in the previous chapter, that short confessional formulas played an important role in the process of tradition
within the periods of both the old and the new testaments.
Such formulas were the ancestors of the christian creeds.
Today, the term 'article of faith' is commonly ascribed both
to the constituent elements of the creed and to those solemn
affirmations of christian belief which are usually known as
'dogmas'. This convergence, however, is a very recent
phenomenon. In the present chapter, therefore, we shall offer
an historical outline both of the creed and of the concept of
'dogma'. Until the strands eventually become intertwined we
shall, within the discussion of each historical period, treat
first of 'dogma' and then of the creed.

In the Septuagint, the word 'dogma' was used, as it was in
the secular Greek of the period, to refer primarily to judicial
decrees, official decisions concerning action to be taken.[1]
In the new testament, the word is not often used, and, when
it is, it usually refers to moral and disciplinary decisions. A
glance at the passages in question serves as a salutary reminder of how dangerous it is to assume that the current
meaning of a term is the meaning which it had at earlier
periods in christian history. 'In those days a decree [dogma]
was issued by the Emperor Augustus' (Lk 2:1; NEB throughout). After the Council of Jerusalem, as Paul and Timothy
'made their way from town to town they handed on the
decisions [dogmas] taken by the apostles and elders in Jerusalem and enjoined their observance' (Ac 16:4). At Thes-
salonica, the crowd 'dragged Jason himself and some members of the congregation before the magistrates, shouting . . .
"They all flout the Emperor's laws [dogmas], and assert that
there is a rival king, Jesus"' (Ac 17:6-7). 'For he himself is
our peace . . . for he annulled the law with its rules and
regulations [dogmas]' (Eph 2:14-15). 'For he . . . has can-

celled the bond which pledged us to the decrees [dogmas] of the law' (Col 2:14). 'By faith, when Moses was born, his parents hid him for three months . . . they were not afraid of the king's edict [dogma]' (Heb 11:23).

In the new testament, there is nothing which can strictly be called a 'creed', but we do find (as we have already noticed) short confessional formulas, such as 'Jesus is Lord', and many instances of what Kelly describes as 'fragments of creeds' (cf Kelly [1960] pp 13–23). We also find fragments of liturgical hymns, such as Philippians 2:5–11, which are doctrinally very rich.

During the patristic period, the term 'dogma' is quite frequently used, and with a wide range of meanings. Sometimes it retains the sense of 'decree', but this is now widened to include revealed injunctions. For example, 'Love your enemies' is a 'dogma' (cf Rahner [1969b] p 205). For Basil, the *kerygmata* are the doctrine of the church in so far as this has been officially declared, while the *dogmata* are those traditions and doctrines which have not been fixed in writing (206). Occasionally, the fathers do use the term to refer to the totality of christian doctrine but, at the same time, they also use it of false doctrine. Augustine, Ambrose, Leo the Great and Gregory the Great almost always use it of heresies, and never of catholic teaching.

The complexity of the early history of the creed is due to the fact that faith was confessed, by individuals and communities, in different contexts in response to different needs. For the sake of simplicity, we shall concentrate on three of the situations in which confessions of faith were employed: liturgical worship, baptism and church teaching.[2] In all three contexts, a double impulse gives rise to the confession of faith. On the one hand, the need of christian faith to situate itself—positively or negatively, affirmatively or polemically—in relation to the human culture and society in which it lives. On the other hand, the need of christian faith to express its praise of and trust in God (cf Jossua [1972] p 50).

Worship. 'To God who alone is wise, through Jesus Christ, be glory for endless ages! Amen' (Rom 16:27). Thus Paul ends his letter to the Romans with a confession of faith in the form of praise, or doxology. Fundamental to the confession

of christian faith is the fact that not only is it structured *as* an
act of worship, but also that one of the contexts in which it
regularly occurs is *in* an act of community worship, as a
liturgical form. It is true that the creed, as a specific formula,
was only introduced comparatively late into the celebration
of the eucharist. But as early as the second or third century
the eucharistic prayers were professions of faith in the form
of acts of praise or worship (cf Jossua [1972] pp 50–51).

It is important to notice how many of even the most elementary doxologies were more or less explicitly trinitarian in
structure (eg, 'Glory be to the Father . . .', and the phrase
from Romans, quoted above). As such, their scope is not this
or that isolated feature of christian belief, but the *whole* of
christian doctrine: 'They constitute a kind of crystallisation
of the creed expressed in worship' (Brekelmans [1970] p 35).
The mystery of the Trinity is not, fundamentally, the object
of one particular doctrine 'alongside' others. It is the one
mystery to which the whole of christian faith and experience
refer. To confess the Trinity is to confess what de Lubac refers
to as 'le Tout du Dogme' (de Lubac [1948] p 156). Nevertheless, the explicitly trinitarian structure of the fully developed creeds and the great eucharistic prayers may obscure
the fact that 'Proclamation of Christ is the *starting-point of
every Christian confession*'.[3] The christian affirmation arises out
of the experience of life in the Spirit of Christ, in which the
Lordship of Christ—which points beyond to the mystery of
the Father—is confessed. Moreover, like the Jewish prayer-
forms from which they were derived,[4] the eucharistic prayers
are confessions of faith in which praise springs from the
people's memory and expresses its hope.

Baptism. At least by the middle of the second century, the
confession of faith on the part of a candidate for baptism took
the form, as it still does in our own day, of his 'I believe', his
'Yes', in response to the questions put to him by the minister
administering the sacrament, questions which again highlight the trinitarian structure of christian confession. The
context is, once again, an act of worship. The candidate's
confession, his 'I believe', is not directly a theoretical assertion that this or that state of affairs is the case (although some
such assertion is implied). It goes deeper than that. It is still,

fundamentally, an act of personal commitment to the God who invites the neophyte to share the memory, hope and way of life of his covenant-people. The dialogue between the minister and the candidate is a microcosm of the covenant-dialogue between God and man.

The dialogue form was not, of course, the only form of confession of faith employed in the baptismal liturgy (taking that term to refer also to the liturgy of the catechumenate). There was, at least from the fourth century onwards, also the rite of the *redditio symboli*, in which a declaratory form was used (cf Kelly [1960] pp 30–38). The creed which we know as the Apostles' Creed, which achieved its final form in the sixth or seventh century, was descended from the form of confession of faith used in the rite of the catechumenate by the church of Rome. The fact that it is in the singular, rather than the plural form, is due to its origins as a pre-baptismal confession of faith.

Doctrine. 'By "doctrinal creed", traditionally called the *symbolum fidei*, we understand a concise formulation of the teaching of faith, which may claim a certain completeness. Such a creed has its origin and function in the framework of religious instruction, apologetics and the fight against heresy' (Brekelmans [1970] p 39). (The Apostles' Creed clearly fits this description; we included it in the previous section because of its close association with the liturgy of baptism). It was the use of the creed as *regula fidei*, as a framework for religious teaching, that led Newman to say that it consisted of 'heads and memoranda of the Church's teaching' (Newman [1836] p 187). Hanson accuses Newman of confusing 'the rule of faith with the baptismal creed' (Hanson [1962] p 65). According to Hanson, 'the rule of faith . . . was not a creed . . . [it] was simply an account, divided into subjects, of the content of the preaching and teaching of the Church contemporary with the writer' (p 93). But this is perhaps unduly to restrict the use of the concept of 'creed'. It is true, as the distinctions we have been employing indicate, that the baptismal confession of faith and the *regula fiedi* are independent in origin. It is also true, however, that the two functions eventually coalesced. Thus, for example, although the Apostles' Creed was, as we have seen, originally used in the context of the liturgy of baptism, it came to be widely employed as a general *regula fidei* as well.

The purpose of the ancient doctrinal creeds was 'to make clear and summarise the Gospel at a certain moment in a particular situation at a particular historical conjuncture. This is most apparent of the Nicene and Athanasian Creeds, which presuppose the christological and trinitarian controversies of the fourth and fifth centuries. But even in the case of the Apostles' Creed, dogmatic controversies of that kind can in many cases be shown to be presupposed by it' (Beirnert [1972] p 73). In other words, any credal formula is 'particular', not only in the sense that it was produced in one cultural and linguistic context rather than in another, but also in the sense that it always more or less deliberately represented a *reaction* by the church against theological tendencies which were felt to threaten the apostolic faith. There is an element of reactive interpretation in any creed. In the case of a formula deliberately drawn up to regulate some doctrinal controversy (as in the case of the Nicene Creed), this element of interpretation can be said to be the dominant concern of the compilers.[5] Thus it came about that the doxological function of the confession of faith was gradually overlaid by the regulative function. A clear indication of this is to be found in the fact that the creed drawn up at the Council of Chalcedon, unlike the earlier forms of it produced at Nicea and Constantinople, never found its way into the liturgy.

'Prior to the beginning of the fourth century all creeds and summaries of faith were local in character' (Kelly [1960] p 205). We tend, today, to think that uniformity of credal terminology throughout the church is necessary in order to maintain unity of belief. We shall have occasion, in a later chapter, to question this assumption. For the moment, it is sufficient to notice that the move towards the imposition of a uniform credal formula, throughout the Roman empire, from the fourth century onwards, was due rather to political pressure from the imperial government than to a doctrinal concern on the part of the church authorities (cf *Concilium* [1970] p 205).

Moving from the patristic era into the medieval period

we find that the term 'dogma' is now rarely used. When medieval theology speaks of what today we would call a 'dogma' it generally uses the concept of the *articulus fidei*. At least until the beginning of the thirteenth century, only those propositions were regarded as 'articles of faith' which formed part of the *regula fidei* as contained in the creed or *symbolum* (cf Rahner [1969b] p 208). Thus it is at this period that the hitherto separate paths followed by 'creed' and 'dogma' begin to converge and form part of a single story.

Throughout the middle ages, the legend that the 'twelve articles' of the creed were composed, one article each, by the apostles, 'won almost universal acceptance' (Kelly [1960] p 3). It died hard. Challenged by several scholars during the fifteenth century, it was 'thrust into the background by the greater controversies of the Reformation' (p 5) and was only disposed of in the seventeenth century. Although historically untenable, the legend bore witness to the abiding conviction that the Apostles' Creed is an authentic summary of the faith handed down from the apostles (cf de Lubac [1969] p 53).

'Lack of knowledge of history, and above all of the pre-history of the apostolic *symbolum*, led theologians of the Middle Ages to regard the *symbolum* as the all-embracing *articulus* (or "joint") of faith around which the totality of dogma turned as a necessary assumption or as proceeding essentially from it' (Schillebeeckx [1967] p 231). Even when, as we have seen, the concept of an 'article of faith' came also to refer to pro-positions other than those contained in the Apostles' Creed, the link between the two was maintained. Only those pro-positions are referred to as 'articles of faith' which express fundamental aspects of revealed truth not reducible to some other element in the content of tradition. Thus in sharp con-trast to the usage with which we have become familiar in modern times, for medieval theology the criterion according to which a doctrinal statement was classified as an 'article of faith' was the centrality of its content in the christian mystery as a whole (cf Rahner [1969b] p 210).

Although medieval theology retained a strong sense of the symbolic nature of doctrinal and credal statements, the em-phasis gradually shifted from a conception of credal language as *medium fidei* (explicitly evoking the relationship between the believer and God) towards a preoccupation with the language, the 'medium' itself. Whereas patristic theology generally moved within the frame of reference of common-sense language, with its preference for the personal, the concrete, the pictorial, the achievement (and the danger) of medieval theology consisted in the fact that it enabled the christian mind to operate, not only directly, but reflexively; not only 'really', but also 'notionally' (to use Newman's distinction). This shift from 'symbolic' to 'systematic' apprehension began with the great councils; but it only achieved its full development in the middle ages (cf Lonergan [1972a] pp 306–310). 'Undifferentiated consciousness uses indiscriminately the procedures of common sense, and so its explanation, its self-knowledge, its religion are rudimentary. Classical consciousness is theoretical as well as common sense, but the theory is not sufficiently advanced for the sharp opposition between the two realms of meaning to be adequately grasped' (p 84). In referring to credal and dogmatic statements as 'symbolic', my purpose is to draw attention to rather more than their inevitable inadequacy. Christian theology has never fallen into the trap of believing that it can adequately describe the mystery of God. But it is one thing to regard doctrinal statements as inadequate objective descriptions. It is another to regard them primarily as expressing, in image and symbol, man's attempt to articulate his understanding of the mystery of his future in God. We shall return to these topics. Within the limits of the present chapter, I am simply drawing attention to the fact that there occurred in medieval theology a shift of emphasis from the personal and religious to the theoretical and 'scientific'. Because, in Lonergan's words, 'the sharp opposition between the two realms of meaning' was not 'adequately grasped', the seeds were sown both of that rationalism in theology which infected the eighteenth and nineteenth centuries and of the various forms of pietism and pragmatism which were its inevitable antithesis.

The reformers reacted strongly against the tendency to lose sight of the religious, confessional nature of doctrinal statements. 'One might even say that [Luther] rediscovered the confessional and doxological function of the creed and rein-

forced it with the composition of hymns to give expression to
the faith' (*Concilium* [1970] p 137). The tradition of keeping
the confession of faith rooted in the context of worship remained a strength of the protestant tradition. We find it
reappearing, for instance, in the rich doctrinal content of the
Wesleys' hymns.

By the time of the Council of Trent, the term 'dogma' is
once again in frequent use. This may to some extent have
been due to the enormous influence exercised, during the
reformation debates, by the *Commonitorium* of Vincent of
Lerins. In view of the fact that 'he is the champion of extreme
conservatism',[6] it is ironic that his idiosyncratic use of biological analogies (with all their inherent ambiguity) should
have led to his being regarded as a pioneer in the understanding of dogmatic development. In a famous phrase,
which will later be canonised by Vatican I, Vincent said that,
while understanding and knowledge of divine mysteries grow
in the church, this understanding is of the same dogma, the
same meaning, the same pronouncement.[7]

But if the term 'dogma' returned to popularity as a result
of Vincent's influence, what did it mean at the time of Trent?
The first and most important thing to notice is that there is
still no question of its being precisely defined. It referred,
broadly and flexibly, to a fixed rule, or an established truth or
fact; to church traditions or to features of ecclesiastical discipline. It indicated that the regulation, truth or custom in
question could be trusted to protect, and not to undermine,
the soundness of ecclesiastical belief and practice. It by no
means referred exclusively to 'revealed truths'. The principal
mark of a *dogma fidei* consisted in its universality. At Trent,
'dogma' was synonymous with 'pertaining to faith', that is to
say, *esse contra positiones Lutheranorum* (Rahner [1969b] p 212,
following Fransen). In other words, the frame of reference
within which the term 'dogma' was used was as wide as its
correlatives 'faith' and 'heresy'. 'The faith', at the time of
Trent, 'could stand for all that a Catholic should in conscience hold' (Bévenot [1962] p 29), including the 'acceptance of ways of conduct which the Church authorities . . .
might lay down' (p 30). Thus, ' "fides" is not formally connected with Revelation as such, as it will be later at Vatican

ı' (Fransen [1972] p 20). Similarly, 'heresy at the Council of Trent was not necessarily reduced to matters of doctrine, and less so to matters of revealed doctrine, but was also related to the universal traditions and customs (*consuetudines ecclesiasticae*), especially in relation to sacramental life' (p 18).

We have already seen how the doxological, confessional function of the creed gradually came to be overlaid, almost supplanted by, its interpretative function in reaction against heresy. This tendency is very marked by the time of Trent: 'The unfortunate result of this mixing of the confessional with the doctrinal is that interpretations become items to be believed, and so the doctrinal interpretation and expansion becomes an object of faith' (*Concilium* [1970] p 137). As a result, the range of propositions that can, in principle, be classified as *de fide*, is now endless. As recently as 1924, Marin-Sola could claim that all rigorously argued theological conclusions in Aquinas' *Summa Theologica* could be defined as *de fide* (cf Marin-Sola [1924] ii pp 55–59).

In the modern period, until very recently, there has been almost total neglect—on the part of 'official' catholic theology—of the doxological, and hence truly confessional nature of credal and dogmatic statements. The emphasis was placed almost exclusively on the intellectual, cognitive component in the act of faith, and in the propositions which faith affirmed. We have seen how flexible the notion of 'dogma' has been for most of its history. In fact, 'the notion of "dogma" only became a technical term in modern times, and in its present meaning only dates from the end of the eighteenth century' (Kasper [1967] p 74). Even after that, the broader meaning survived for several decades. Thus Pius ix, using the inevitable passage from Vincent of Lerins in his letter *Singulari Quidem*, in 1856, 'does not use dogma in its present precise theological sense but rather as a synonym for religious and even sometimes philosophical truth' (McGrath [1953] p 73).

By the eighteenth century, an old world had died. There was no longer any confident, living unity and co-inherence of life, faith, worship and doctrine. Many new questions were asked, new methods of inquiry introduced. As a result, the 'pieces' of the old world became something of an embarrass-

ment. Creeds and dogmas became isolated from life and faith
(is this not still the situation today? how many christians
'believe', in any religiously significant sense, in the ascension?). With the rise of historical theology, which insisted on
the autonomy of its norms and procedures, traditional dogmatics came to be regarded as little more than an arbitrary
manipulation of the 'pure gospel' on the part of ecclesiastical
authorities. From here it is a short step to the view that
'dogma' is the illegitimate fruit of the corruption of christianity under pagan, 'hellenising' influences, a point to which
we shall return (pp 104ff).

Unfortunately there was a tendency, so far as catholic
theology was concerned, to accept the terms of the debate,
and to lay increasing emphasis, in the defence against 'historicism' and 'rationalism', on the formal authority of declarations by ecclesiastical authority. We saw, in the previous
chapter, the same tendency at work in the gradual 'shrinkage'
of the concept of 'tradition' until it came to be identified with
magisterium. Thus the criterion according to which a doctrinal statement was classified as an 'article of faith' came to
be, not so much the centrality of its content in the christian
mystery as a whole, but rather the degree of solemnity,
authority or certainty with which it had been proposed for
belief by the appropriate authority (cf Rahner [1969b] pp
214–218).

As we shall see when we discuss Newman's *Essay on
Development*, this shift of emphasis is reflected in the wide-
spread nineteenth century charge that the catholic church
had 'added to' or 'expanded' the creed. It is true that, in
recent centuries, several doctrinal propositions not contained
in the creed have been classified, on the highest authority, as
propositions to be held *de fide*. It is also true that 'professions
of faith' were drawn up by the Council of Trent, at the time
of the modernist crisis, and in our own day by Paul vi with
his 'Creed of the People of God'. Nevertheless none of these
formulas was introduced into the liturgy and none of them
was recognised by the church as supplanting the ancient
creeds. Thus it is that, in spite of the ambiguity which currently attends the concept *de fide*, as a result of the shift in
emphasis to which we have drawn attention, when one refers

today to 'the creed' one is still understood to be referring to
the ancient confessions of faith, apostolic or niceno-con-
stantinopolitan.

The final stage that we need briefly to consider in this historical sketch is the first Vatican Council's treatment of
dogma and its immutability in the constitution *Dei Filius*.
The quotation from Vincent of Lerins on the 'growth' in the
church's understanding of the 'deposit', to which we have
already drawn attention, was incorporated into the text, but
whereas Vincent understood by 'dogma' the entire content of
the tradition, the *depositum fidei*, Vatican 1 clearly distinguished between the 'dogma' and the 'deposit'. The 'deposit'
consists in the content of revelation, whereas 'dogmas' are
authentic authorised and infallible declarations of the word
of God in the church, especially (but not exclusively) those
declarations which take the form of solemn judgements or
decisions, on the part of the *magisterium* (*ibid* p 218 following
Geiselmann). This concept of 'dogma', which still has overtones of its original Greek sense of 'decision' or 'edict', is
in discernible continuity with the medieval concept of *articulus
fidei*, once the field of applicability of that concept had been
broadened, in the thirteenth century, beyond the confines of
the creed, to include other authoritative declarations of
christian truth.

It is true that, confronted by the 'rationalism' of the period,
Vatican 1 was primarily concerned to insist upon the autonomy of christian truth, and hence the authoritative nature
of solemn ecclesiastical declarations. But, 'apart from the
authoritative character of dogma Vatican 1 also stressed its
relativity. The Council made a clear distinction between the
Gospel, the deposit of faith, and the ecclesiastical formulation
of doctrine, the dogma. The dogma is but an analogous, inadequate, human statement of the divine truth' (Kasper
[1967] p 76). But once this important distinction has been
drawn, it becomes necessary, for the first time, to ask whether
and in what sense such human statements share in the
immutability of divine truth.[8] Thus the problem is set up,
which will explode in the modernist crisis: what is the relationship between the word of God and these words of man?
The council contented itself with asserting the permanence

of the meaning of dogmas: *Hinc sacrorum quoque dogmatum is sensus perpetuo est retinendus, quem semel declaravit sancta mater Ecclesia*' (Denzinger, 1800). The 'meaning of the dogma is not apart from a verbal formulation, for it is a meaning declared by the church. However, the permanence attaches to the meaning and not to the formula. To retain the same formula and give it a new meaning is precisely what the third canon excludes . . . it seems better to speak of the permanence of the meaning of dogmas rather than of its immutability' (Lonergan [1972a] p 323).

There is no point in attempting to summarise this rapid survey of the history of the creed and of the concept of 'dogma'. It is, however, worth drawing attention to one feature of this history: namely, the tendency increasingly to concentrate on one aspect of an originally rich and complex reality. Greater differentiation and precision is often won at the cost of considerable impoverishment of meaning. We saw, in the last chapter, that something similar is the case where the history of 'tradition' is concerned. But whereas the concept of 'tradition' has, in recent years, recovered much of its original richness without loss of conceptual precision, the same can hardly yet be said of the concept of 'dogma', or authoritative declaration and confession of christian belief. This is partly due to the pressure, since Vatican I, which a particular concept of 'infallibility' continues to exert. We have still a long way to go before we can give a satisfactory account of the way in which authoritative declarations of christian belief are to be related to other aspects of our christian experience and historical understanding. From one point of view, it could be suggested that the problem of 'doctrinal development' is a problem of responsibly relating to our christian past in such a way that we are able to confess our faith today, without either repeating dead formulas or reducing that confession to a mere declaration of existential attitudes. These are questions to which, in the light of the historical data which we have now accumulated, we must turn in the next chapter.

NOTES

1. In this chapter, I shall make extensive use of Rahner [1969b]. The English translation (*Kerygma and Dogma*, trans W. Glen-Doepel [New York, 1969]) is not very useful since it omits, without warning, much of the historical material.

2. We are here following Brekelmans [1970]. For a more detailed analysis of the situations that generated confessions of faith, see Cullmann [1949] p 18; Kelly [1960] pp 13–14.

3. Cullmann [1949] p 39. This does not, I think, necessarily contradict Kelly's observation that, even where fragments of credal material in the new testament are concerned, 'the Trinitarian pattern which was to dominate all later creeds was already part and parcel of the Christian tradition of doctrine' (Kelly [1960] p 23; for his criticism of Cullmann, see pp 25–28).

4. Cf the early chapters of Bouyer [1966]. This rich mine of insight and information is marred by the fact that Bouyer has too many axes to grind.

5. This is true even if the dominant motive at, for instance, Nicea, was one of compromise. To decide to compromise is to take a decision.

6. Walgrave [1972] p 88. Walgrave goes on: 'Vincent does not like the idea of development . . . If one takes account of his own rigorism in interpreting his canon, one cannot avoid the conclusion that the principle of development does not fit in with it. There is a contradiction between the canon as he understands it and the idea of development. This latent contradiction will work itself out in later history. The *Commonitorium* will meet with a great and lasting approval and will be the refuge of both conservatives and progressives' (p 89).

7. 'in suo dumtaxat genere, in eodem scilicet dogmate, eodem sensu eademque sententia'. In the translation, I am following Lonergan [1972a] p 323.

8. In the context, the quotation from Vincent of Lerins amounts to 'no more than an assertion of the fact that dogma does evolve within the limits imposed upon it by its own immutable nature' (McGrath [1953] p 129); a judgement the unsatisfactorily paradoxical nature of which accurately reflects much modern catholic thinking on the problem.

7

QUESTIONS AND REFLECTIONS

Any 'theory' of doctrinal development, or of doctrinal change and continuity is, as Newman said, 'an hypothesis to account for a difficulty' (Dev p 30). The difficulty arises from the conviction of christian belief that the message proclaimed in the life, death and glorification of Jesus Christ is God's definitive word to mankind. Therefore unless the word proclaimed to men of every successive age and culture is, in some significant sense, the *same* word, God's promise is not fulfilled. And yet it is clear that what christians do, and think, and say today is very different from what they did, and thought, and said yesterday—or the day before. Therefore, we need some 'theory' or 'hypothesis' which can, so far as possible, reconcile our conviction concerning the continual availability in history of the unchanging gospel with our recognition of the extent, variety and complexity of historical change. We shall see, when we come to examine the theories of doctrinal development that were elaborated during the first half of this century, that many of them suffered from one fatal weakness: namely, the too rapid imposition of *a priori* theoretical models on the complex data of christian history.

Now, it may be true that the historian cannot be the ultimate arbiter where questions of the truth or validity of religious beliefs are concerned. Nevertheless, if theology consists in reflection on the facts of christian life and experience; if theology is the interpretation of living christian faith, then, although the historian may be denied the last word, he is entitled to the first word: 'The primary requirement of historical theology is that it be good history' (Pelikan [1971] p 129). In the previous two chapters we have been, as it were, 'listening to the history' of the concepts of tradition, creed and dogma. My aim in the present chapter is to do no more than indicate, in an unsystematic way, some of the theoretical or interpretative questions suggested by that history.

In the historical and social sciences, it is axiomatic that, if we wish to understand a statement or event, we must take into account the context in which the statement was uttered or the event took place. Therefore, before undertaking any exercise in hermeneutics, or interpretation, we need to ask: how broad is the relevant context, how wide the range of relevant data?

In view of the fact that, from both an historical and an ecumenical point of view, it is the historicity of dogmatic definitions which is widely felt to pose some of the most difficult problems, it might seem—at first sight—that a study of the 'development of dogma' could restrict itself to solemn pronouncements by popes and councils. But, in view of what we have seen in the previous chapters, this would clearly be anachronistic: it would be to read back into history our rather precise contemporary concept of 'dogma'. For a variety of reasons, 'Any distinction between the history of dogma and the history of theology seems to have become untenable; and at least for the Middle Ages and the 19th century, so, presumably, has any distinction between the history of theology and the history of philosophy' (Pelikan [1971] p 93; cf Lonergan [1967a], p 266, [1972a] pp 337–340). It does not follow, however, that the field of relevant data may be restricted to the statements of the learned. For too long, '*Dogmengeschichte* has concentrated not on the history of what the Church believed, taught, and confessed, but on the history of erudite theology' (Pelikan [1969] pp 46–47). Indeed, following up that hint of Pelikan's, we must admit that the field of relevant data may not be restricted to *statements* at all. Human beings express themselves not only in what they say, but also in what they do: in gesture, habit, social structure, forms of worship, and so on. Therefore, if we wish to discover what the church has believed, we must look not only to what has been said, but also to what has been done. 'We don't think that language, as a form of human expression, must be considered as the highest form of self-expression. Life is more important, and to live we need "patterns of behaviour", which as community-built forms of life . . . are, as it were, the concrete language of our daily behaviour' (Fransen [1972] p 8). There is, therefore, no aspect of the history of the church which may, *a priori*, be declared to be irrelevant to an inquiry into problems of doctrinal change and continuity. It is not, of course, mere coincidence that this preliminary methodological observation connects up with what we have seen (in part 1) to be the dominant concept of revelation in *Dei Verbum* (revelation as the deeds of God in history, and not merely the words that interpret those deeds), and also with what we have seen to be the biblical, patristic and contemporary notion of 'tradition' as the whole process of christian history.

Whatever else we may want to say about the history of tradition (or, therefore, about the history of particular aspects of that tradition); about the history of the creed (or, therefore, about the history of individual articles of the creed); about the history of dogma (or, therefore, about the history of individual dogmas); at least it is certain that the historical process in question is not a thin, straight line, an unswerving trajectory without significant variation or change. And yet some such image has often been (more or less consciously) employed by those who seek to describe doctrinal history as a process of linear deduction from divinely revealed premises. On such an account, the process is presumed to be linear, because it is deductive; it is presumed to be a straight line because the providential guidance of the Spirit of Truth will keep the process 'on the straight and narrow'.

Similarly, it is certain that this historical process cannot adequately be conceived on the analogy of a uniformly expanding cone of Blackpool Rock: wherever you cut it, the image or pattern is substantially the same. And yet, some such image has often been (more or less consciously) employed by those who seek to describe doctrinal history as a process in which the initial message is 'expanded' or 'enlarged' as time goes on.

Thus, for example, we have noticed a tendency for originally rich and complex notions to 'shrink', to be supplanted by more abstract and partial ones, as particular aspects of an originally many-sided and complex idea (such as that of 'tradition') alone survive to command attention. We have also seen that when an originally flexible idea becomes hardened or particularised, it proves unserviceable as

a vehicle for meaning and communication at times of major
cultural change and upheaval. At such times, newly experienced needs and problems lead men to discount, as unhelpful
or irrelevant, the distillations of inherited wisdom. They seek
to appeal directly from the demands of their own turbulent
experience to that original richness embodied in the new
testament. The result is a crisis of theology, a crisis of
authority, and possibly a crisis of faith. Something like this
occurred at the reformation, and has occurred again in the
twentieth century. Whether or not such crises are, on balance, creative or disruptive, whether or not they succeed in
recovering that original richness, and transposing it into the
new situation, may be regarded as an open question. But at
least the occurrence of such crises suggests that, not only is the
history of christian belief and doctrine not a linear process,
an undisturbed conveyor-belt for eternal truth, but that, if
we are to take with sufficient seriousness the discontinuities
of christian history, we may have to integrate the concept of
'revolution', as well as that of 'evolution', into our understanding of the process of doctrinal development.

It would also seem to be the case that the contexts in which
doctrinal decisions are taken, and theological exploration is
pursued, are such as to make it more or less inevitable that
there should be a dialectical element in the history of doctrine: that the path followed by the history of christian truth
should admit 'des cheminements . . . zigzagants' (Congar
[1970c] p 611). Thus for example, authoritative affirmations by popes or councils have usually been negative in
thrust (whether or not this is made explicit by the publication
of canons to which anathemas are attached). From this
point of view, it can be said that 'dogma's primary function . . . is to fence off the ways in which Scripture may not
be interpreted' (Schoonenberg [1970] p 136). This reactive,
dialectical quality of christian doctrine is not only discernible in authoritative pronouncements. It also characterises
almost every movement in theological debate or christian
practice. It follows that, in attempting to arrive today at
some coherent understanding of doctrinal development, we
have to try to take into account whatever it is that, more or
less consciously, we are reacting against. Thus, for example,

such exaggerated claims have been made, in Roman catholic accounts of doctrinal development during the last hundred years, on behalf of the *magisterium* that it would be easy to over-react, and to elaborate a view of the process of the transmission of christian truth in which the holders of apostolic office had no significant function to perform. (It must be admitted that this is not a temptation to which the present holders of such office show much tendency to succumb.)

Recognition of the extent to which the history of tradition has often been, even for long periods, a process of impoverishment rather than enrichment, often induces a certain romanticism in respect of earlier periods in christian history. But if the solution to problems of change and discontinuity is not to be sought in the imposition of abstract models on obdurately complex historical evidence, neither is it to be sought in a nostalgia which is, fundamentally, just as non-historical.

In the first place, the past is, from many points of view, simply irrecoverable. This lesson has often had to be learnt the hard way by liturgists and catechists. 'The poverty of our Christian instruction, and the poverty of our common life, was at first thought to consist in the inadequacy of the *content* of our teaching. The remedy was thought to lie in "getting back to the Bible". It doesn't. It consists in getting back to ourselves'.[1] Our world, our problems, our thought-patterns, may be illuminated and corrected by those of the bible. But the fact remains that our world is simply not the same as the world of the new testament, or the medieval schoolmen, or the fathers of Trent and the reformation.

In the second place, the process of clarification, of asking questions and answering them, while it may entail the loss of a certain child-like innocence, is not only inevitable, but it also brings its own reward. If the early church had not asked questions and answered them, we should not have had the new testament at all. If it had not asked certain questions and answered them, we should have had Mark's gospel, but not John's; the christological hymn in Philippians, but not the definition of Chalcedon.

Moreover, we have seen that, throughout the middle ages right up to the time of Trent, the notions of 'dogma', 'faith' and 'heresy' referred, very broadly and empirically, to just about everything that the church said and did. We would not wish to return to this situation, even if we could. It is undoubtedly an advantage to have more precise, more restricted definitions of such notions, thus enabling us with greater assurance to sort out the fundamental from the peripheral, and not to feel in conscience bound to carry with us the entire furniture of the church's past.

Any study of doctrinal development is concerned with three questions: What has changed? What has remained unchanged? How do we evaluate such changes as have occurred? It may be helpful, at this point in our inquiry, to consider these questions in very broad and general terms. My purpose in doing so is to throw out some preliminary hints; the questions should acquire greater precision and clarity as we proceed.

WHAT HAS CHANGED?

The great majority of the *terms* employed in christian discourse have changed in the course of the church's history. From Aramaic and Greek, through the long centuries in which Latin was the 'official' language of the western church, to the bewildering variety of contemporary languages; there are few vocabularies that have not been employed, at one period or another, for the proclamation of the gospel, confession of faith, and christian worship and instruction.

Somewhat less superficially, many terms have been introduced into christian discourse which were not there (nor were their near equivalents in another language) from the beginning. The classic instance, of course, is the introduction of *homoousios*. We have seen how the term 'dogma' only very gradually came to be employed as a theological term. It is important to remember that when new terminology is introduced into theology or church teaching, it is rarely generated from within specifically christian discourse or concern. Far more often, some term which is already available in the secular language of a period or a culture is put to the service of christian theology. (It may be that, in so doing, its original meaning is 'bent' to new purposes, but for the moment we are only concerned with terms, not with meaning.)

The *rites* of christian worship have varied as dramatically, and as frequently, as has the terminology. By 'rite' I mean not simply the skeletal structure as it appears in a service-book (where these exist), but the whole concrete dramatic phenomenon of sound, light, colour, song, organisation and so on. Considered as 'drama', there is little in common between the rites of, say, penance or the eucharist, as cele-brated in the second, sixth, thirteenth, seventeenth and twentieth centuries. And, once again, this pluralism in styles of celebration is as obvious synchronically as it is diachroni-cally. The Easter liturgy in a Greek cathedral, a student mass in an American university, a lutheran service in a German village, a papal mass in St Peter's: empirically, dramatically, these have little in common.

Nor are forms of worship the only christian institutions which bear striking witness to the pluralism of the forms taken by the process of christian tradition. This pluralism has been equally characteristic of the 'concrete language' of forms of *church order*. It could, indeed, be objected that I have simply been labouring the obvious. But, if the range of relevant data for reflection on problems of doctrinal change and continuity is, as I have claimed, as broad as the whole concrete process of christian history, it may be well to remind ourselves of aspects of that history which too narrow and abstract a con-ception of 'doctrine' or 'tradition' has too often dismissed as 'non-theological'.[2]

Terms change, rites change, institutions change. But what of the *meanings* embodied in these terms, rites and institu-tions? Do not they remain constant, thus providing us with the assurance that eternal truth is not subject to the vicissi-tudes of human history? It is worth pausing to notice how this problem has been tackled by three authoritative catholic pronouncements.

'If any one shall say that it may happen, from time to time, in the course of the progress of science, that a sense may have to be attributed to dogmas proposed by the church other than that which has been and is understood by the church: *anathema sit*' (Vat i, *Dei Filius*, 4; Denz 1818; my trans). It

seems likely, from an earlier draft of this canon of Vatican I,
that the council's conception of the permanence of the meaning of dogmas was somewhat simplistic; that they were working with a concept of immutability which our contemporary
awareness of hermeneutical problems has rendered unserviceable.[3] Nevertheless, the final wording of the canon is quite
compatible with a more sensitive view of problems of historical interpretation (cf Lonergan [1972a] pp 320–326).

According to Paul VI's encyclical *Mysterium Fidei*, dogmatic statements 'may indeed . . . have a clearer and more
obvious exposition, but only with the same meaning as that
with which they were [originally] employed . . . *ut pro-
ficiente fidei intelligentia maneat fidei immutabilis veritas*' (Trans
CTS, 25). While it is true that the pope seems to take for
granted a 'clearer explanation' theory of doctrinal development, his principal concern is simply to affirm the abiding
truth of dogmatic statements. Neither *Dei Filius* nor *Mysterium Fidei* tells us *how* we are to ensure that the meaning originally embodied in a dogmatic statement is to be appropriated in a new cultural, linguistic and epistemic context.
They merely insist (and Vatican I's formula seems happier
than Paul VI's) that that which the church has solemnly declared to be true remains permanently true; they neither
solve nor prejudge those problems of interpretation which
have become particularly acute in our own day. And we have
already seen, in part 1, that *Dei Verbum* restricted itself to
affirming that we expect no new public revelation since the
coming of Christ (art 4), and that, assisted by the Spirit, 'The
Church . . . tends perpetually towards the fullness of
divine truth' (art 8).

Language does not possess a meaning 'on its own'. Words
only mean what people mean when they use them. When we
say that someone is using a word incorrectly, we mean that
he is ignoring or rejecting the appropriate canons of meaning.
But those canons of meaning, which regulate what a given
society means by particular words, can change.

Thus, for example, we have seen that the meaning of words
such as 'tradition', 'dogma' and 'faith' has changed considerably in the course of christian history. We have also seen
the shift from a use of credal language in which the confes-

sional or doxological meaning was dominant, to a situation in which the confessional meaning of the articles of the creed was, in practice, virtually lost sight of, and in which the now dominant descriptive meaning had shifted from the symbolic or 'mythological' to the literal.

Finally, just as changes in terminology, rite and institution seem to have owed at least as much to 'secular' linguistic, cultural and social factors as to any directly or dominantly theological concern, the same can be said of the changes in the meaning embodied and expressed in that terminology, those rites and institutions. What has changed? The answer seems to be: everything. There is no aspect of christian life, structure and language that is immune from the process of history. 'The reference of Christian faith to history unavoidably carries with it the demand that the believer must not try to save himself from historical-critical questions by means of some "invulnerable area"—otherwise it will lose its historical basis' (Pannenberg [1970b] p 56).

WHAT HAS REMAINED UNCHANGED?

In sketching an answer to this second question, we shall make use of the same four categories: terms, rites, other institutions, meaning. If we ignore (which, in this context it is safe to do) the problem of translation from one language to another, we notice that there are some unchanged terms. Significantly, these terms refer to particular historical facts: people, places, events. Christian discourse has always referred to the same nucleus of historical fact: to Jesus, to his death, to Jerusalem, and so on.

So far as rites are concerned, the element of continuity seems to reside in that aim or intention which dictates the overall structure of the rite. Thus, if we take the example of the eucharist, the church has always *assembled*; its worship has been understood to be a public, communal activity. It has assembled to hear the word of God; the reading and interpretation of the scriptures has been a constituent element of the eucharistic liturgy since apostolic times. (The concept of 'interpretation' should not here be understood, narrowly, to refer only to verbal preaching. In the orthodox liturgies, for example, the rites that surround the proclamation of the gospel clearly 'say' that this word that is read is no mere passage from a book, but is the voice of Christ, the word of God, crucified and risen.) Thirdly, the church has always sought to *respond* to the word in the *sacrificium laudis*; the church's obedient 'Yes' to God's covenant-invitation, affirmed in the taking, blessing, sharing and eating of bread and wine.

So far as other institutions are concerned, it is not unimportant to notice that the church has never been an entirely unstructured community, and that amongst the variety of offices exercised in the church, there have always been those whose task it is to represent the apostolicity of the church, both in time ('apostolic succession') and in space ('communion' between churches; and in this context, mention should be made of the existence, from early in the church's history, of the office of the primacy, the principle of unity of faith and communion: cf *Constitution on the Church*, 18).

Our glance at the extent to which meanings have changed in the course of doctrinal history has shown how difficult it is to put one's finger on that sense in which 'the same' meaning has been expressed, in successive cultural contexts, in different languages, rites and institutions. Because this, above all, is a problem to which we shall have to return in later chapters, a few general suggestions will, at this point, have to suffice.

In the first place, let me suggest that the element of continuity of meaning is to be sought in the area of concern, or intention. In using its languages, rites and institutions, the church has been guided by a formally invariant aim or intention, which could be expressed in various ways: 'to hear the word of God and keep it'; 'to follow Christ'; to affirm that the cross of Christ is the key both to the mystery of human existence and to that ultimate mystery which we call God.

It is important to notice how crucial the factual element in the christian confession becomes at this point. What the church has sought has not simply been that liberation for which men long, or that revolution in self-understanding which transforms them. It has sought to affirm, in the light of the mystery of Christ, that such liberation, such self-understanding, is possible. It has affirmed Christ as saviour. It is

Jesus and his death to which christian confession points as to its centre; of which all christian doctrine and instruction attempts to be the celebration, defence and interpretation.

But have we any ground for affirming that the interpretation which we place upon the cross today is, in any significant sense, the same as that placed by earlier generations, and above all, by the originating witness of the apostolic church? The interpretation of documents, the study of doctrinal history, can, inductively, point to features held in common by two or more such interpretations (and can also help us to discover the discontinuities in christian history). But, in the last resort, the affirmation that there is a significant continuity of christian meaning rests on the affirmation of faith, of trust in God, that the interpretation which we put upon the cross is not simply a figment of our creative intelligence, but is rather something that is given to us in the gift of God's Spirit.

We have been brought back to the definition of revelation which I offered in chapter 2: a definition in which the divine warrant for man's interpretation of certain events as salvific was as important as the ascription of those events to the hand of God. Thus to say that revelation continues in the church does not mean that earlier interpretations (and, above all, those embodied in the new testament writings) can now be discarded, or declared to have been false. To say that revelation continues in the church is to affirm, in faith, that the Spirit continues to assist us, in different personal, linguistic and cultural contexts, to 'hear' the event of Jesus' life, teaching and death as the one word of God to man.

HOW DO WE EVALUATE CHANGE?

We saw, in chapter 4, that *Dei Verbum* insists on the interdependence of scripture, tradition and *magisterium*, but that it casts very little light on the problem of the normative roles to be ascribed, in practice, to these three components of that historical structure by means of which the word of God is authoritatively proclaimed in the church. But at least it can be shown that it is unsatisfactory to attach exclusive authority to any one of these components. (We have already briefly mentioned these three unsatisfactory solutions in chapter 4.)

The programme *scriptura sola* affords no solution in so far as this is understood in a fundamentalist manner that denies all authority to subsequent christian history and to present belief and teaching. It affords no solution, in the first place, because it is unworkable. What one man regards as the 'obvious'meaning of a passage of scripture is often by no means obvious to the next man. There is no possibility of rationally escaping from the hermeneutical problem; from the task of critical interpretation. It affords no solution, secondly, because the new testament is, as much as any other collection of human writings, a product of history. There is no evidence that the authors of the new testament ever intended their writings to be used in such a manner.

The programme 'tradition alone', or 'history alone', is equally unsatisfactory. If the first unsatisfactory solution is the result of allowing respect for the authority of the new testament to get out of control, and to give way to 'bibliolatry', this second solution is the result of allowing our trust in God's providential guidance of history to get out of control, and to give way to an idolatry of historical process. On this account, whatever has happened has happened for the best, and binds us simply because it *has* happened. Whatever the church has said or done is claimed to be the providentially guided interpretation of scripture, however improbable this may seem to the exegete. We can recognise here the perspective within which some of the more bizarre theories of the 'senses of scripture' were elaborated, and within which the cruder forms of 'proof-texting' have taken place.

It is one thing to confess one's faith that God will ensure the survival of the gospel message, and that he will therefore also ensure the survival of the message-bearing community. It is quite another thing to refuse to recognise, in spite of the clear evidence of history, that survival is compatible with considerable malfunction, deformation and disease. The old testament is always there to remind us that the survival of God's people, and of the promise which they remember, celebrate and proclaim, is compatible with a history as chequered and uneven as that of any other community.

Finally, the ascription in practice of unique normative

significance to 'what we have done for a long time' is incompatible with theoretical claims concerning the primacy of the scriptural witness to God's word in Christ.

At a time of massive, perhaps unprecedented, cultural, social and scientific change and upheaval, it is perhaps not surprising that many people should opt for the third unsatisfactory solution, that of ascribing unique normative significance to the *present* belief and understanding of the christian community (we might call this 'today alone', to distinguish it from 'scripture alone' and 'history alone'). It is interesting to notice that the tendency to succumb to this temptation is shared by 'radicals' and 'conservatives' alike. The radical may espouse it in the name of 'relevance', the conservative in the name of his confidence that whatever the pope, for example, teaches or directs today is to be regarded as authoritative simply because the pope has taught or directed it.

Perhaps the most pervasive context in which christians have tended to ascribe supreme normative significance to 'today' has been that in which the characteristic cultural stance is one of uncritical confidence in human and christian progress. To this we shall return when discussing the modernist crisis.

The insistence of *Dei Verbum* that scripture, tradition and the contemporary experience and understanding of the church are to be regarded as interdependent will be fruitful to the extent to which we eschew the temptation to seek deceptively simple solutions, and are prepared to live with the tensions that necessarily result from treating each of these three factors with appropriate seriousness. And because in recent centuries we have, as catholics, tended in the direction of the second and third unsatisfactory solutions, our current need is still to shift the emphasis in the direction of the first. As Walter Kasper has said: Vatican II 'certainly emphasises the interconnection of Scripture, tradition and magisterium, but their interrelation is no longer a one-way process. It is no longer a question of interpreting Scripture in the light of tradition and dogma, but the biblical scholar is now expected to make his contribution to the Church's judgement. This means that the process may be inverted so that dogma must be understood in the light of Scripture' (Kasper [1967] p 77).

Is there any framework within which our understanding of

the relationship between scripture, history, and the authority of 'today' may be synthetically presented? I believe that there is, and that it is to be found by turning to the liturgy, and noticing that the pattern of christian celebration is still, as it has ever been, a pattern of *anamnesis*. We saw in chapter 5 that, in the life of the early church, as in the period of the old testament, those events in the community's past in which it recognised the saving hand of God, or (which amounts to the same thing) which it interpreted as having revelatory significance, were recalled in the present in the conviction that they still spoke to the present (however different that present might be, and therefore however difficult it might be to apply the lessons of the past), and spoke to it of that future, that promise, held out to man in the past by God.

In other words, it is the church's task in every age to seek so to relate to its past (which means, above all, to its originating moment, definitively witnessed to in the new testament), as to enable that past, interpreted in the present, effectively to function as a challenge: a challenge to look, and think, and trust, and act in the direction of that future which is promised to us in the new testament.

NOTES

1. Moore [1967] p 145. For a more technical elaboration of this insight, notice the insistence on the centrality of christian experience as the starting-point of theology in Lonergan [1972a]; an insistence that has led one commentator to refer to him, with less than complete accuracy, as 'the Catholic Schleiermacher'.

2. A few years ago, I drew attention to Clark's study of late medieval eucharistic theology as a striking instance of this methodological weakness: see Lash [1968] pp126–129.

3. The draft read: 'Quare si quis dixerit, talem admittendam esse intelligentiae dogmatum explicationem per humanae rationis et scientiarum progressum, ut ille sensus, quem ecclesia in suis definitionibus suaque articulos fidei propositione intellexit et intellegit, non semper et incommutabiliter verus sit, sed secundum profectum scientiarum iisdem definitionibus et propositis fidei articulis aliquando alius diversus sensus substitui debeat, anathema sit' (Petit [1924] col 67).

8

MAGISTERIUM: FROM FUNCTION TO FUNCTIONARIES

Frequent reference has been made, in earlier chapters, to the concept of *magisterium*. But to what, or to whom, does the term refer, and what does it mean? It is certainly not my intention even to attempt an outline history or theology of teaching authority in the church. This is a vast subject, on which a great deal has been written in recent years. The problem of authority is, however, closely bound up with the problem of doctrinal development. This will become clear when we discuss modern theories of development. At this stage, all that I propose to do is to focus on two historical aspects of the problem: firstly, a change in the meaning of the term *magisterium*, which took place during the nineteenth century; secondly, the famous clause *ex sese, non autem ex consensu Ecclesiae* of Vatican i.

The connection between these two aspects of the problem may be illustrated from the problem of *Humanae Vitae*. We saw, in chapter 4, that although the insertion of the phrase *pie audit* into article 10 of *Dei Verbum* was of considerable importance, it did not solve the problem of where, or how, the *magisterium* should listen for the word of God. For many people, the most disturbing feature of *Humanae Vitae* consisted in the fact that the pope felt free to reject the advice given to him by the commission which he had appointed and that, in doing so, he claimed that obedience was due to 'the Magisterium . . . less for the reasons given for decisions, than from the fact that shepherds in the Church enjoy the Holy Spirit's special guidance' (quoted Harris [1968] p 154). The implications of this claim were more disturbing than the effect of the encyclical on the agonising problem of birth control, because there seems no reason why the pattern should not repeat itself on some future occasion.[1]

If we go back several decades, we discover the following by

no means unusual statement in a commentary on the decree *Lamentabili*: 'The Pope and the bishops . . . can consult the sources of faith directly; when they debate in council, or when they prepare their definition, they can bypass any private work which has already been done on the question: and this all the more in that they possess, I do not say new revelations, but a special assistance of the Holy Spirit, which not only prevents any erroneous definition (a negative result), but which positively guides their work and applies their minds' (Harent [1909] col 608; my trans).

In both cases, there is a conscious dissociation of the *magisterium* from what the rest of the church may be believing and thinking, which not only seems almost to place the pope and other bishops outside the church, but which does so in a manner which is tantamount (in spite of verbal disclaimers) to regarding them as the recipients of some private revelation.

Moreover, if one were to say that the authoritativeness of *Humanae Vitae* could not accurately be gauged until the reaction of the church as a whole had been taken into account, one would probably be reminded of Vatican I's assertion that dogmatic definitions are irreformable *ex sese, non autem ex consensu Ecclesiae*. (Paul VI did not regard any part of his encyclical as satisfying Vatican I's conditions for such a definition, but he is only one of many catholics who tend to model their view of 'lesser' papal pronouncements on their understanding of the teaching of Vatican I.)

Catholic tradition undoubtedly asserts that Christ's divine authority continues in the church through apostolic succession. 'But has the authentic teaching function come to be restricted exclusively, in a way which is neither primitive, necessary, nor proper? I suggest that it has, and comparatively recently'.[2] The word *magisterium* means 'teachership', which is a function. But the modern use of the word designates functionaries, and does so in a restricted sense which excludes all but pope and bishops. Robert Murray suggests that this shift was, for a long time, not noticed by theologians, precisely because nobody denies that divine authority is vested in these functionaries. But, in so far as the shift has led to a denial that authentic teachership has been given to the church as a whole, and is validly exercised by many, it is unfaithful to the mainstream of christian tradition.

In the early church, the bishops saw their relationship to the *magisterium* (teachership) of Christ as consisting in a responsibility to ensure that there was sound teaching in their churches. From this point of view, our modern tendency to think of bishops, and especially the pope, as teachers in a sense which excludes the rest of the church, has lost sight of the original meaning of 'episcopacy', or 'supervision'. From an etymological angle, it is worth noticing that, from the thirteenth century onwards, a distinction was made between the 'authoritative' or 'authentic' sayings (*dicta authentica*: passages from the scriptures or the fathers), and 'teacher-sayings' (*dicta magistralia*: passages from the writings of theologians).

During the middle ages, the increasingly sharp distinction between 'clergy' and 'laity' led, eventually, to the verbal identification of 'the church' with the clergy. The middle ages also saw an increasing tendency, as we noticed in chapter 5, to conceive of church authority in terms of power 'handed over' by God to the holders of apostolic office. It also became increasingly common to conceive of the relationship of God to church councils in terms of 'vertical contact' (cf Congar [1966] p 178) amounting to a form of inspiration.

The Council of Trent 'did not even use the word *magisterium*' (p 181). In the post-reformation period, we have already seen how the concept of 'tradition' contracted until it was virtually identified with one of the organs of tradition: namely, the episcopate and, especially, the papacy. During the early nineteenth century, the increasing status accorded to the papacy in respect of other bishoprics (a shift often brought about by the episcopate itself in an attempt to ensure freedom from political control),[3] led to a new phenomenon in the life of the church: the promulgation of frequent papal encyclicals.

Although the distinction between 'the teaching church' and 'the taught church' was by now firmly established, the term *magisterium* was still being consistently used to refer to a function in the church. At some point in the mid-nineteenth century, the term began to be used to refer also, and eventually exclusively, to a particular group of functionaries in the church: the pope and the other bishops. The difference between the two usages is strikingly similar to that between references to the function of 'government', and to a particular group of political functionaries: 'the government'. In view of this shift in meaning, and of the survival of 'vertical contact' models of the relationship between God and ecclesiastical office-holders, it is not difficult to see how the assumption could emerge that such office-holders could appeal to a 'special assistance' of the Holy Spirit as a sufficient warrant for their pronouncements and decisions.

In recent years, the theological pendulum has begun heavily to swing back in the opposite direction. This swing is indicated by the overall structure of Vatican II's *Constitution on the Church* and, in particular, by the fact that, in a passage echoing Pius XII's encyclical *Humani Generis*, the council omitted a clause to the effect that, once the mind of the pope was known on a hitherto disputed question, that question could no longer be regarded as a matter of free debate amongst theologians.[4]

The publication of *Humanae Vitae*, and of Hans Küng's study of infallibility, together with the debate stimulated by both documents, shows just how confused the discussion of teaching authority in general, and of 'infallibility' in particular, has become.[5] Infallibility language has got out of focus. We want to believe that the truth of Christ is taught in the church, but the language of infallibility now makes this harder, rather than easier. 'All ways gradually force us back towards the Orthodox idea that an authoritative statement must be recognizable by the Church and accepted by the Church' (Robert Murray, cf note 2).

On 18 July, 1870, the first Vatican Council promulgated the constitution *Pastor Aeternus*, which ended with the words: 'and therefore such definitions of the Roman Pontiff are irreformable of themselves, and not from the consent of the Church'.[6] This phrase, the most notorious in the *Constitution*, was taken up and repeated, a century later, by Vatican II (cf Constitution on the Church 25).

It is important to bear in mind the social, religious and political climate in which Vatican I took place. 'In the spiritual crisis of the time, in contradistinction to the philosophical systems which were ranged against Christianity and offered a substitute for religion, and not least of all in view of the hardly hopeful prospects before the ecclesiastical centre in Rome, a strengthening of this very centre seemed necessary and inevitable' (Conzemius [1971] p 82). As Mgr Nardi, auditor of the Roman rota, wrote shortly after the council opened: 'any government which cares about its survival ought to thank God that its subjects believe in an infallible Pope, because he who believes in the Pope believes in God, and he who believes in God never conspires to overthrow a government'.[7]

The major theological weakness of the debates at the council was the juridicism of its ecclesiology. As a result, the discussion of infallibility tended to operate within legal perspectives. For example: do papal acts, to be authoritative, ie valid, require legal ratification by the other bishops? Moreover, although 'Gallicanism, Jansenism and Josephinism had expired long ago as effective spiritual movements' (Conzemius [1971] p 75), the debate on infallibility was directed against gallicanism and, especially, against the fourth gallican article of 1682, which had claimed: 'In questions of faith the Pope has the chief part, and his decrees apply to all the churches and each church in particular; yet his judgement is not irreformable unless the consent of the Church be given to it' (quoted Butler C. [1930] i, pp 27–28).

On 11 July 1870, Bishop Gasser of Brixen, who 'stands out as the most prominent theologian of the Council' (ii, p 134), presented the report of the doctrinal commission on amendments to the draft chapter on infallibility. Commenting on complaints that the draft (which did not yet include the phrase: *non autem ex consensu Ecclesiae*) was separating the pope from the rest of the church, he said: 'We are not separating the Pope, we are not in the least separating the Pope from the consent of the Church, provided that such consent is not understood to be a condition, whether antecedent or consequent . . . This consent [of the Church] can never be lacking [to papal definitions]'.[8]

Two days later, a general vote was taken on the third and fourth chapters of the draft and the following day, 14 July, the doctrinal commission met to consider last-minute amendments recommended in the *modi* to that vote. On 16 July, Bishop Gasser reported back to the council. When it became clear that, at this eleventh hour, the *non autem* clause had been added, there was uproar. The council minority felt betrayed. The following day, Cardinal Rauscher of Vienna went to see the pope. According to the official report of the minority group, he begged Pius ix to examine the matter personally, reminding him of the danger that would result if what was a mere opinion of a theological school was defined as of divine faith. The pope replied that he had not got time to deal with the matter (cf Thils [1969] p 121). The next day the constitution *Pastor Aeternus* was solemnly promulgated.

It is clear from the debates, and especially from Bishop Gasser's reports, that the phrase was concerned with the legal conditions that need to be verified before a solemn dogmatic definition is known to embody an infallible judgement. The phrase is not concerned with the manner in which the pope ought to reach his decision. It is certainly not saying that the pope can teach whatever he feels like teaching, or that the papacy is the primary locus of that sharing in the infallibility of Christ with which 'the divine Redeemer wished to endow his Church' (Denzinger 1839). According to Gasser, formal consultation of the episcopate could not be built into a dogmatic definition as a *sine qua non* condition, because there are 'other private ways, which suffice for full information' (quoted Butler C. [1930] ii, p 139). Gasser clearly took it for granted that 'full information' was necessary. It was simply assumed (as is evident from the passage, quoted above, in Gasser's report of 11 July) that consent, agreement, would not be lacking. In other words, the council trusted—perhaps naively —the orthodoxy and prudence of the pope. The phrase 'is about the criteria for recognizing the lawful force of [the Pope's] pronouncements, not about how he comes to formulate them' (Murray [1968] p 39).

It is therefore unjustifiable to appeal to *Pastor Aeternus* in support of the view that recognition, 'reception' by the church as a whole is not a normal and normally necessary feature of the articulation of dogma in the life of the church, and an important theological criterion by means of which a dogmatic statement may be recognised as such.

Newman was one of those who regretted the definition because he regarded it as unnecessary, and because he felt that it had been too hastily executed, insufficient attention being paid to the historical problems. Some time later Lord Acton reflected on Newman's reaction: 'In 1870 he announced that he would accept whatever the Council should decide. In . . . 1871 he startled Loyson by saying: Crescit in dogma. The old idea had revived. He was waiting for the echo' (Cambridge University Library, Additional MSS, 4989.3). That 'echo' was the reception of the christian people, their recognition that a doctrine propounded by accredited teachers in the church represented, in fact, the faith of the church.

NOTES

1. This explains why Hans Küng felt it appropriate to devote an entire chapter of his recent study of infallibility to the encyclical: cf Küng [1971] pp 27–52.

2. Throughout this section, I shall be making extensive use of unpublished notes and papers by Robert Murray, from whom that remark is quoted. I am deeply grateful to him for permission to use this material.

3. A similar concern played an important part in the escalating papalism of the high middle ages: cf Meulenberg [1972].

4. Compare the second paragraph of art 25 of the *Constitution on the Church* with the last sentence of paragraph 20 in the CTS edition of *Humani Generis* ('False Trends in Modern Teaching').

5. For a good summary of the debate generated by Küng's book, see Hughes [1971]; one of the most helpful contributions to the debate was Congar [1970c].

6. 'ideoque ejusmodi Romani Pontificis definitiones ex sese, non autem ex consensu Ecclesiae, irreformabiles esse' (Denzinger 1839).

7. ' "un gouvernement tant soit peu soucieux de sa propre conservation, devrait rendre grâce à Dieu de ce que ses sujets croient en un Pape infaillible, car qui croit au Pape croit à Dieu, et qui croit à Dieu ne conspire jamais pour renverser un gouvernement" ' (quoted from Thils [1969] pp 65–66).

8. ' "Demum papam non separamus, et vel minime separamus a consensu Ecclesiae, dummodo consensus iste non ponatur ceu conditio, sive sit consensus antecedens sive sit consequens . . . Hic consensus numquam ipsi deesse potest" ' (quoted from Groot [1966] p 816; cf Butler C. [1930] ii, p 137).

PART THREE

NEWMAN, MODERNISM AND BEYOND

9

NEWMAN ON DEVELOPMENT

According to Jaroslav Pelikan, Newman's *Essay on Development* is the 'almost inevitable starting-point for an investigation of development of doctrine' (Pelikan [1969] p 3). Paradoxically, although few studies of doctrinal development fail to make passing reference to the pioneering status of the *Essay*, it has rarely been subjected to detailed and serious study. 'Members of the charmed circle of German Lutheran historians of dogma relegated Newman to a footnote or treated him as nothing more than the ancestor of a doomed Roman Catholic Modernism' (Pelikan [1971] p 58). It is the modernist crisis, above all, which accounts for the suspicion and misinterpretation to which the *Essay* was subject, for half a century, in catholic theology. In Newman, an almost excessively cautious temperament and an unswerving commitment to what he called the 'dogmatic principle' (the principle, that is, that God's truth is prior to man's attempts obediently to respond to that truth in faith, holiness, and 'that loving inquisitiveness which is the life of the *Schola*' (Dev p 337), went hand-in-hand with a profound recognition of the fundamental changes in religious awareness and theological method which were demanded by that revolution in epistemological and historical consciousness which Lonergan describes as the shift from a 'classical' to an 'empirical' culture (cf Lonergan [1968]; [1972a] pp ix, 29, 300–302). The modernists recognised in Newman a man who had felt the pressures of problems with which, sooner or later, catholic thought would have to come to terms. One of the most lucid and balanced summaries of the main arguments in the *Essay* was written, in 1898, by Loisy [1898] who, two years earlier, had referred to Newman as 'le théologien le plus ouvert qui ait existé dans la Sainte Eglise depuis Origène' (quoted Vidler [1934] p 94).

In the aftermath of the modernist crisis, Newman's *Essay*

was either ignored, as suspect,[1] or 'tamed' by being read through the interpretative filters of neo-scholasticism. Newman must be shown to be orthodox. Therefore he was not a modernist. Therefore he must have been, in some sense, a thomist. The tentative, empirical, inductive patterns of argument in the *Essay* were ignored. Newman was presented as the author of a systematic, abstract 'theory' of doctrinal development: 'it was John Henry Newman . . . who finally formulated a comprehensive theory of doctrinal evolution' (Bent [1969] p 11). The best advice for someone who wishes to understand Newman's *Essay* is to ignore the commentators (including this one!), and to concentrate on the *Essay* itself (its contemporary significance is assessed in Lash [1971b]).

Newman has long been acknowledged to be a master of English prose. But the implications of this have often been ignored (especially on the mainland of Europe) by interpreters of his theology and philosophy. If you summarise a poem, and say: What the poet meant was . . ., you have lost the meaning of the poem. In Newman's prose, meaning and style, meaning and method of argument, are so closely interwoven that any attempt to separate them is a hazardous undertaking. His lack of any systematic and technical terminology, in most of his writing, is irritating to a certain temper of mind, which cannot appreciate the possibility that, even for a thinker of Newman's delicacy and precision, the unit of meaning may be the paragraph, or the page, rather than the individual term. Literary and scientific precision are not necessarily the same thing.

Secondly, it is important never to lose sight of the concrete, personal nature of his writing. His suspicion of abstraction and generalisation arises from the fact that, always writing from his own personal experience and conviction, he writes for another person, real or imaginary: *Cor ad cor loquitur*. He is, first and foremost, a controversialist, who seeks to persuade you to share his point of view, rather than a theoretician concerned to 'prove' or 'demonstrate' an abstract conclusion: 'Logic makes but a sorry rhetoric with the multitude; first shoot round corners, and you may not despair of converting by a syllogism' (D.A. p 294).

'Like its predecessor the Evangelical Movement, [the

Oxford Movement] was more a movement of the heart than
of the head . . . It always saw dogma in relation to worship,
to the numinous, to the movement of the heart, to the conscience and the moral need, to the immediate experience of
the hidden hand of God' (Chadwick [1960] p 11). Newman
always retained a strong sense of the religious, confessional,
symbolic nature of dogmatic statements. Nowhere did he
express this more forcefully than in the essay on the Arian
controversy, first published in 1833. There he criticised those
who, in the fourth or the nineteenth century, used 'the
figurative terms of theology in their literal meaning' (Ari p
34). In a passage with characteristically neoplatonic overtones, he suggested that 'the systematic doctrine of the
Trinity may be understood as the shadow, projected for the
contemplation of the intellect, of the Object of scripturally
informed piety: a representation, economical; necessarily
imperfect, as being exhibited in a foreign medium, and
therefore involving apparent inconsistencies or mysteries'
(Ari p 145). And, in a phrase which strikingly summarises the
shifts in epistemological perspective which we discussed in
chapter 6, he said: 'We count the words of the Fathers, and
measure their sentences; and so convert doxologies into
creeds', and this the pressure of doctrinal controversy has
forced us to do 'more or less from the Nicene Council down-
wards' (Ari p 180).

The *Lectures on the Prophetical Office of the Church*, published
in 1837, are the supreme achievement of Newman's anglican
theology. These lectures, the ecclesiological charter of the
Oxford movement, assert the normative status of scripture as
interpreted by the church of the first five centuries. After this
period, in which the central doctrines of christological and
trinitarian belief were articulated in the great creeds, no
radical development is necessary or possible. For their motto,
the lectures appeal yet again to Vincent of Lerins' *Commonitorium*: 'The Rule or Canon which I have been explaining, is
best known as expressed in the words of Vincentius of Lerins
. . . that that is to be received as Apostolic which has been
taught "always, everywhere, and by all"' (V.M.1 p 51).

On the one hand, Newman attacks protestantism for
abandoning the principle that scripture is rightly heard only

if interpreted in the community of the church, and for replacing it with the principle of 'private judgement'. On the
other hand, he judges Roman catholicism to be 'corrupt',
because it has 'added' new dogmas to the ancient creeds, thus
abandoning the rule of antiquity, and because it has allowed
a gulf to grow between its theory and its practice.

By 1841, his confidence in the theoretical foundations of
anglicanism had been shaken. In the Advent of that year, he
preached four moving and beautiful sermons 'on the safety
of continuance in our communion' (S.D. p 308; nos xxi–xxiv,
pp 308–380). Because he was no longer certain that the
anglican church possessed the 'external notes' of a true church,
he emphasised the internal 'tokens' of the presence of Christ:
'What are signs and tokens of any kind, but the way *to*
Christ? what need of *them*, should it be so, through his mercy,
that we have found Him? who asks his way when he has got to
his destination? why seek the shadow, if we already have the
substance? why seek him elsewhere, if we have reason to trust
we have found Him here?' (S.D. p 319). The emphasis is in
need of correction, but these sermons eloquently illustrate
Newman's preoccupation with the role of living faith, of
holiness, in any adequate conception of 'orthodoxy'.

In 1843, he delivered the last of his *University Sermons*, on
'The theory of developments in religious doctrine' (U.S. pp
312–351). This sermon has often been regarded as a sort of
preliminary sketch of the *Essay on Development*. In fact, although they have features in common, notably the reliance
on the analogy between the growth of truth in an individual
mind and in a society (cf Lash [1970] for difficulties in
Newman's treatment), the two works are very different, and
it is not surprising that the sermon is only once quoted in the
Essay. Whereas the framework of inquiry in the *Essay* is primarily historical, in the sermon Newman is chiefly concerned
(as in the other *University Sermons*) with the relationship
between 'faith' and 'reason',[2] and between 'implicit' and
'explicit' reasoning in religious belief.

Between 1839 and 1845 a number of factors, personal,
temperamental, historical and doctrinal combined to bring
about a gradual shift in Newman's ecclesiological viewpoint.
The outcome of this slow process of shifting perspective, or

changing 'view', was the intuitive, imaginative conviction that 'the Roman Catholic Church' was the answer to 'the simple question . . . Where, what is this thing in this age, which in the first age was the Catholic Church?' (Diff 1 p 368). But the ground of his previous charge of corruption remained, as an obstinate 'difficulty'. Before he could bring himself to change his denominational allegiance, he had to persuade himself that his new 'view' admitted of argumentative justification. Hence the *Essay on Development;* hence the fact that it remained unfinished: it had done its job.

If, anywhere in the *Essay*, there is a summary of its central apologetic judgement, it is here: 'Did St Athanasius or St Ambrose come suddenly to life, it cannot be doubted what communion he would take to be his own' (Dev pp 97–98). Newman simply takes it for granted that, if there is a revelation, if there is *one* revelation, if that revelation's maintained public availability even to the unlearned is guaranteed by divine providence, then there must be, somewhere in the world today, an authentic, adequate and authoritative embodiment and expression of that revelation. The question then becomes: how do I decide which amongst existing contenders is that embodiment of revelation? Newman proposes to answer this question by means of an appeal to history. But here he runs up against a difficulty. He had formerly appealed to history to justify the anglican position. If he now wishes to make such an appeal on behalf of the Roman catholic church, he must both find a flaw in the argument he had employed in the *Lectures on the Prophetical Office* and overcome what had previously seemed the crucial weakness in the Roman claims: namely, the apparent lack of identity between the Roman catholic church and primitive christianity. It is not surprising, therefore, that the weight of the historical analysis in the *Essay* should be on the side of the search for continuity, rather than on the recognition of discontinuities, in christian history.

The heart of his critique of the *Via Media* is as follows: it is evident (and he had previously been at pains to point this out) that there was development of doctrine and life in the early centuries. By why stop at the early councils? Is it not arbitrary to claim that significant doctrinal development came to an

end with the formulation of the great creeds? The canon of
Vincent of Lerins 'admits of being interpreted in two ways: if
it be narrowed for the purpose of disproving the catholicity
of the Creed of Pope Pius [IV], it becomes also an objection to
the Athanasian; and if it be relaxed to admit the doctrines
retained by the English Church, it no longer excludes certain
doctrines of Rome which that Church denies' (Dev pp 11–12).
He insists that he is not rejecting the Vincentian canon; he is
merely pointing out that, in practice, it is unworkable: 'The
solution it offers is as difficult as the original problem' (Dev
p 27). But, if the Vincentian canon is unworkable, we have
need of another 'hypothesis', or 'theory', by means of which
to interpret the facts of christian history.

   Those who read the *Essay* expecting to find a systematic
and unified theory of doctrinal development, in the twentieth-
century sense, either find what is not there, or else are disappointed. In our own day, we simply take it for granted that
the church, in its doctrine, life and structure, has in some
sense 'evolved', 'developed' or 'changed' throughout the
course of its history (however we evaluate the changes that
have taken place). Newman did not share this assumption.
It was the *fact* of 'development' which he offered as an
'hypothesis', as an alternative to 'immutability', on the one
hand, and 'corruption' on the other. He took into consideration many widely differing types of development, both because
the complexity of the historical evidence demanded this, and
because his heuristic conception of 'development' as the key to
the problem was not further implemented in the form of
any single 'theory' of development, in the modern sense,
at all.

   His aim was specific and restricted. He was not trying to
'demonstrate' that this or that body is the authentic heir to
primitive christianity: the *Essay* '*is not written to prove the truth*
of Catholicism . . . but to answer an *objection against*
Catholicism' (L&D XII p 332). In 1849, regretting that he was
unable 'to construct a *positive* argument for Catholicism', he
wrote: 'The negative is most powerful—"Since there must
be one true religion, it can *be none other* than this"' (L&D XIII
p 319). Failure to advert to this aspect of Newman's method
has led many commentators to assume (catholics with joy,

protestants with sorrow) that the *Essay* attempts to prove from history that the highly centralised, authoritarian Roman catholicism of the mid-nineteenth century represents the only possible 'true development' of the christian 'idea'. Yet, again and again, in his letters, Newman insists that he did not join the catholic church because he came to believe in the papacy, but accepted the papacy because he came to believe that Roman catholicism represented the one 'real', 'living' embodiment of the christian 'idea'.[3] Similarly, the form of argument in the sections on 'An Infallible Developing Authority' (Dev pp 75–92), and 'The Papal Supremacy' (Dev pp 148–165), might give the impression that Newman regarded the papacy of Pius ix as the ideal form of church government. Anyone familiar with Newman's life, and especially his later writings around the time of the Vatican Council (which yet precede his revision of the *Essay* in 1878), knows how far this is from the truth. He is here, as usual, arguing negatively; making out a persuasive apologetic case for the claim that the existing doctrine and practice of the Roman church are not necessarily 'corruptions'.

So far, I have been concerned to indicate some features of Newman's method of argument which suggest that those who appeal to the *Essay* in support of non-historical theological theories of doctrinal development are unwise to do so. Now, more positively, I propose to comment on the historiographical method which Newman adopted in the *Essay*.

What Newman needed, and what he sought to provide in the *Essay*, was a 'view' of christian history: 'When we have lost our way, we mount up to some eminence to look about us', we don't 'plunge into the nearest thicket to find our bearings' (L&D xi p 69). The only 'method by which we are enabled to become certain of what is concrete' is by 'the cumulation of probabilities' (G.A. p 127). Hence the crucial role played, in the *Essay*, by arguments from 'antecedent probability'. Chapter two argues that it is antecedently probable that doctrine will develop, and that there will be, in the church, an 'infallible developing authority'. Chapter three is a defence of the method which has thus been put to use. Chapter four tries to show what the early evidence looks like if the argument of the preceding chapters is accepted. For

Newman, an argument from antecedent probability is not the imposition of a preconceived theory upon the evidence, but a more or less well-founded claim that it is reasonable to expect that, in a particular case, the data bear witness to one state of affairs rather than to another. In our own day, when we have become very conscious of the impossibility of 'presuppositionless' historical interpretation, and when even philosophers of natural science speak of the 'theory-laden' nature of scientific data, the formal validity of such a methodology hardly requires demonstration.[4]

According to Newman, christianity, since it 'consists of men . . . has developed according to the laws under which combinations of men develop' (Ess II p 196). Unlike those theologians whose interpretations of doctrinal history owe far more to theology than to history (and who thereby seek to immunise their theories from historical criticism), Newman insists, in a long passage in the first edition which he later omitted,[5] that the method of historical interpretation which he employs 'is no peculiarity of Catholic and orthodox reasoning, but is equally found in infidel and heretic' (Dev 1845 ed, p 183). However, while Newman refused to rely on any peculiarly 'religious' or 'theological' method of interpreting doctrinal history, he strongly criticised those historians who misused a sound method in a reductionist manner which would eventually render christian belief impossible. According to Newman, 'what is historically human may be doctrinally divine' (Ess II p 230). So, while christian belief should never inhibit us from taking the risk of studying history *as* history, neither should the historian systematically exclude the possibility that human history may be patent of theological interpretation. But it must be an historically plausible interpretation, not the imposition of religious convictions on the evidence of the past.

In chapter 7, I argued that there is no aspect of the history of the church which may, *a priori*, be declared irrelevant to a study of doctrinal development. One of the more striking features of the *Essay*, in contrast to most catholic studies of doctrinal development, consists in the fact that the range of data to which, in principle, Newman appeals, includes all aspects of the church's life, thought, structure and experience.

In principle only because, in practice, the apologetic nature of the *Essay*, and the limitations of Newman's own competence and interest, seriously reduce the effective range of data. One of the weaknesses of the *Essay* (as of much modern Roman catholic ecclesiology until very recently) lies in its espousal of a concept of the *unity* of the church which cannot acknowledge 'ecclesial reality' in any denomination other than the Roman catholic church. A study of doctrinal development which cannot admit that 'it is quite as just to conceive of a development of *all* Christianity as a development of the Roman Church' (Butler W. A. [1850] p 175), cannot be expected to cast much *direct* light on our contemporary hermeneutical problems.

Newman is notoriously erratic, and often uncritical, as an historian. In drawing attention to those aspects of his method which are relevant to the problems with which we are concerned in this book, I am not suggesting that his performance as an historian was on a level with the genius of his methodological insights.[6]

The most famous passage in the *Essay* is the closing sentence to the section 'On the Process of Development in Ideas': 'In a higher world it is otherwise, but here below to live is to change, and to be perfect is to have changed often' (Dev p 40). In this important section, explicit references to christianity are rare. This is no accident. Consistent with his historical method, Newman does not appeal directly, or exclusively, to doctrinal considerations. He presents what we have called the process of tradition, phenomenologically, as an instance of the history of 'living' and 'real ideas' in society at large. For Newman, a 'real idea' is not sharply differentiated, ontologically, from the 'object' which it 'represents': it *is* that object, as perceived, apprehended, grasped, in the life and thought of a society. Throughout the section, the *unity* of the 'idea', as of the 'object', is taken for granted. The process described is that of the 'warfare of ideas under their various aspects' (p 39), as men struggle, under the pressure of events and of the tension between different 'aspects' of truth, less inadequately to express and to embody the truth which moves them.

What, in Newman's view, is the 'idea' of christianity? In order to answer this question, it is necessary to bear in mind the extent to which Newman's patterns of description are 'fugal' in structure. The discussion is always moving at several levels at once. In the present instance, while on the surface the section presents a general phenomenological account of the growth and development of 'ideas' in a society, at a deeper level its reference is not merely ecclesiological, but specifically christological. The 'idea' in question is that of revelation, of God's self-disclosure in history. The reason why, by the end of the section, the 'idea' seems to be an objective entity, existing independently of and influencing the minds of men, is that there is an implicit reference to the presence in history of the risen Christ, God's living word.

It is not difficult to see that the broad theological perspective within which Newman is operating is closer to the theology of revelation and tradition in *Dei Verbum* than it is to preconciliar neo-scholastic catholic theology. Any 'theory' of doctrinal development depends, in the last resort, upon the conception of revelation that underlies it. We must therefore ask some rather more precise questions about Newman's view of the relationship between the revelation made in Christ and doctrines explicitly appropriated and defined at later stages in the church's history.

According to Owen Chadwick, 'If it were established (for example) in Catholic theology that "revelation ended with the death of the last apostle", Newman's theory could hardly survive without a restatement so drastic as to leave it almost unrecognisable' (Chadwick [1957] p 160). We have already seen, in part 1, that this formulation of the definitive nature of the revelation made in Christ has been superseded in catholic theology. But we cannot leave the matter there. Chadwick also claims that, according to Newman, the 'original revelation . . . was given partly in explicit doctrines, partly in feelings which were left to be subsequently drawn out into doctrines' (p 157). This is, in effect, to attribute to Newman a 'two sources' theory of revelation of which there are indications in some of his earlier writings but which, in the *Essay*, is resolutely subordinated to his insistence on the *unity* of the 'idea'. Part of the difficulty arises from the fact that Newman's treatment of revelation in the *Essay* would have gained in coherence if he had more clearly perceived that the categories within which the christian claim to the finality of the

Christ-event were, at the time, expressed, were inadequate to their intention (cf Misner [1970]).

One of the devices which Newman employs to make good the claim that later doctrines are the explicit appropriations of 'aspects' of the one 'idea' is an analogy between the fulfilment of prophecy and the development of doctrine: 'Thus too we deal with scripture, when we have to interpret the prophetical text and the types of the Old Testament. The event which is the development is also the interpretation of the prediction; it provides a fulfilment by imposing a meaning' (Dev p 102). He claims that the later stages in the history of prophecy and its fulfilment (within the biblical era) were 'contained within' earlier prophetic utterances, and yet were later stages in the *revelation*. The *'effata* of Our Lord and His Apostles are of a typical structure, parallel to the prophetic announcements' (Dev p 66). On what principle can one deny to the 'developments', in word and event, of these *effata*, the status of further revelation? This is a problem which Newman never satisfactorily resolved. Thus, for example, if the only sense in which the papacy can be said to have 'existed' in the world in the early centuries was as an 'unfulfilled prophecy' (Dev p 150), would it not be simpler to say of the papacy what Newman's colleague at Oriel, John Davison, said of christianity as a whole: 'There was a time when Christianity was not in the world, but only foretold: a time when it had no being, but in prophecy'? (Davison [1861] p 278).

In common with many writers on the history of ideas, Newman takes it for granted that the process of thought in the mind of an individual provides an analogy for the development of an 'idea' in a society. But where the development of doctrine is concerned, the analogy has only limited value. Throughout his life, Newman insisted that growth in holiness is a necessary condition of growth in the knowledge of God. The safeguard of faith is, in the last resort, not credal, liturgical or institutional forms, but a life of loving obedience. Newman was surely correct in stressing the ethical component in the religious apprehension of truth. But, in view of this, it would seem possible to claim that the contemporary church had a deeper grasp of God's revelation than had the primitive church only if, at the same time, it could be claimed that the church had grown in holiness. For all his confidence in the providential guidance of the church, few ideas would have been more foreign than this one to Newman, who 'never believed in progress' (Chadwick [1957] p 97).

We shall see, in a later chapter, that for several decades after the modernist crisis, the only theories of doctrinal development which were admitted in catholic theology were those which purported to discern, in the history of doctrine, a process of 'homogeneous evolution'. And it became fashionable to attribute this concept to Newman, as one of its pioneers. In fact, the *term* 'homogeneous' is rarely used by Newman, and never in the *Essay*. It is true that the view that the process of development is homogeneous, expanding and irreversible has a significant place in his argument. But, once again, we must remember that his aim is apologetic, rather than explanatory. You say that the Roman catholic church is corrupt? Very well, show me where the corruption has entered in (cf Dev pp 5–6, 99, 135, 169, 206). The purpose of such passages is to support a persuasive argument to the effect that, if you look at the history of christianity from a certain point of view, it has not really changed that much at all! Moreover, there are other passages which show that Newman was not unaware of the dialectical aspect of doctrinal history (cf eg Dev pp 36–39, 439).

The claim that the process of development is a process of 'homogeneous evolution' has often gone hand-in-hand with a disturbingly literal use of organic models. And these, once again, are usually fathered on Newman. Thus Lindbeck refers to 'cumulative, organic growth theories which derive from Cardinal Newman' (Lindbeck [1970] p 101), and Echlin observes that 'The linear, organic view that has been so prevalent since Mohler and Newman is yielding to theories of doctrinal development based on historical self-understanding' (Echlin [1970] p 10). It is true that it was 'on the analogy of biology that Newman hit upon his seven notes or tests of genuine development' (Davis [1967] p 186), but, in Newman's hands, it remains an analogy, and not an 'organic theory' of the development of doctrine (note the explicit rejection in Dev p 41). Far from a biologistic interpretation of historical process leading Newman to interpret that process in organic terms, it was rather his conviction that the church, indwelt by the Spirit of the risen Christ, uniquely 'lives', that led him to employ organic imagery to describe its history.

There is one other feature of the *Essay* on which, in this chapter, it will be useful to comment. Any suggestion that dogmatic statements are 'irreformable' would seem to imply that such statements represent the *term* of an aspect of the process of development. On Newman's account can, and does, the process of development reach a term? A comparison of the *Essay* with the last of the *University Sermons* suggests the following answer.

In so far as the development of individual doctrines is concerned, Newman does seem to envisage a point at which their development reaches a term: for example, the doctrine of original sin is said to be 'completed' or 'fully developed' at the time of Augustine (cf Dev pp 126–127, 129) Both the overall development of the christian 'idea', and the development of particular doctrines, are envisaged by Newman as two-stage processes. The first stage is the development from implicit (that is, non-reflexive) awareness to explicit articulation in a body of doctrine. The second stage is the further elaboration and expansion of that body of doctrine.

From one point of view, the general process reaches a term, inasmuch as the emergence of the creed may be regarded as an 'exact and complete delineation' (Dev p 52), or linguistic microcosm, of the 'idea'. From another point of view, it can never do so: there are no signs of the general process 'coming to an end' (Dev p 29) and 'complete delineation' remains an ideal.

So far as the history of particular doctrines is concerned, Newman undoubtedly recognised that dogmatic statements have a subsequent history of interpretation, adjustment or 'explanation', but he underestimated their historically conditioned nature, and he explicitly rejected the possibility of their being 'reversed' (cf Dev p 202; Diff ɪɪ p 307).

NOTES

1. It is symptomatic that, as late as 1951, the papers of a Roman congress on doctrinal development (published in *Gregorianum* xxxiii [1952] pp 5–182; xxxiv [1953] pp 182–237) should contain only one passing reference to the *Essay*.

2. It is important to bear in mind that Newman regularly uses these terms, not in their ordinary usage, but to refer to contrasting epistemological styles or, as he says, 'habits of mind'.

3. Cf L&D xi pp 174–175, 190, 238, 239; L&D xiii p 301; L&D xiv pp 354, 360–361, 365–368, 369–372; L&D xv pp 19, 39, 41–42; L&D xx pp 304–309; and so on.

4. Thus, according to one commentator, the notion of 'antecedent probability' plays a similar role in Newman's thought to that played by the 'Horizont des Verständnisses' for Husserl, or 'Vorverständnis' for Bultmann: cf Willam [1969] p 39.

5. Why did Newman omit this passage (which runs from pp 182–202 in the 1845 edition) from the revised edition? According to Chadwick, the omission 'illustrates a marked feature of that revision—the partial restatement or removal of the appeal to history' (Chadwick [1957] p 149). Quite apart from the fact that Newman retained passages which contained the essential argument, there is a simpler explanation; as F. D. Maurice wrote in 1846: 'All Mr. Newman's doctrine about the nature of evidence may be granted . . . Were more than sixty octavo pages required to prove points which seem not to advance the argument one step?' (Maurice [1846] p xlviii).

6. The best recent assessments of Newman as an historian are a series of studies by J. D. Holmes: cf eg Holmes [1970].

10

NEWMAN: PROBLEMS OF AUTHORITY

'It is never enough . . . to show that later doctrine is a development of earlier. Our search is for criteria which will enable us to say why one development is true and another false, or even why one development is in some respects truer than another' (Wiles [1967] p 168). In chapter 7, we outlined three unsatisfactory answers to the question: How do we evaluate change? At first sight, it might seem that Newman's answer is to be found in the provision, in the second part of the *Essay on Development*, of the seven famous 'notes' or 'tests' of a 'true' or 'genuine' development. If we looked there, we should be disappointed. It is true that, taken together, the tests do have a certain coherence. But they are not (as they have often been taken to be) general criteria for distinguishing sound from unsound developments. Fundamentally, their purpose is not criteriological, but apologetic: 'they rather serve as answers to objections brought against the actual decisions of authority, than are proofs of the correctness of those decisions' (Dev p 78). It would, however, be a mistake to assume that those contemporary critics of the *Essay* were correct who claimed that Newman had simply abandoned the authority of scripture and antiquity, ascribing to the words and deeds of present authority alone any effective normative significance. Nevertheless, there are two features of Newman's handling of problems of authority which give such critics grounds for suspicion.

In the first place, although Newman was too sensitive to the complexity of history and the incomprehensibility of divine providence to have been a determinist, there is a strand of argument in the *Essay* which laid him open to the charge of assuming that the '*mere historical eventuation* of dogmas . . . is a sufficient evidence of dogmatic *truth*' (Butler W. A. [1850] p 81). But this feature of the *Essay* is, once again, the result of Newman's apologetic efforts to persuade the reader favourably to view such developments as had taken place in the history of Roman catholicism.

In the second place, there are puzzling references to an 'external' developing authority. Thus, for example, if 'it is probable that some means will be granted for ascertaining the legitimate and true developments of Revelation, it appears . . . that these means must of necessity be external to the developments themselves' (Dev p 78). To point to the practical necessity of an authenticating function, or *magisterium* in the church, is one thing; to claim that such an authoritative office must be 'external to the developments themselves', is quite another. How could such office be immune from that historical process of development to which all 'aspects' of the 'idea' are necessarily subject? After all, many passages in the *Essay* are devoted to arguing that the historical development of forms of authority in the church have been 'true' developments. This problem is by no means of merely historical or academic interest. According to one of the most learned of recent studies of doctrinal development, a study heavily influenced by Newman, 'the social reality of the Christian community must have an *external* spokesman' (Walgrave [1972] p 308, my stress; cf p 383). A few pages later, Walgrave refers to 'a doctrinal authority that *externally* guides the Church' (p 310, my stress). This is ecclesiologically intolerable. It is a regression to a conception of church authority which is tantamount to placing the pope and the other bishops outside the church; a view to which we briefly referred in chapter 8.

In order to understand Newman's references, in the *Essay*, to an authority 'external to the developments themselves', it is necessary to look back at the theology of tradition contained in his anglican writings. By the time that he wrote the *Lectures on the Prophetical Office*, he was distinguishing clearly between 'Episcopal' and 'Prophetical Tradition'. From one point of view, the former, which is 'received from Bishop to Bishop' (V.M. 1 p 249), has as its content the 'fundamentals' of christian doctrine, contained in the creed and the liturgy. From another point of view, however, it contains, embodies and safeguards the entire revealed 'deposit', that 'deposit' which is '"dilated in Scripture, contracted in the Creed"'

(Abp Bramhall on the 'Rule of Faith', quoted from V.M. II
p 278). The concept of the prophetical tradition, on the
other hand, refers to the whole rich complexity of the life,
teaching and worship of the church, which is seen as 'existing primarily in the bosom of the Church itself, and recorded
in such measure as Providence has determined in the writings
of eminent men' (V.M. I p 250), and in the 'Decrees of
Councils' (V.M. I p 254).

In the anglican writings, the content of the 'Episcopal
Tradition' is frequently described as 'external' to the individual believer in the sense that, being expressed and embodied
in creed and rite, it is 'objectively', publicly available. The
key to the puzzling references, in the *Essay*, to an authority
'external to the developments themselves', lies in the fact
that, in such passages, the 'authority' in question is the
'Episcopal Tradition'. The process of development is presumed to take place in the 'Prophetical Tradition', and to
culminate, in some instances, in the incorporation of the
term of the development, by solemn ecclesiastical decision,
into the 'Episcopal'. It can be shown, if one reads the *Essay*
in conjunction with Newman's writings on tradition not only
before, but also immediately after its publication, that the
basic structures of his anglican conception of tradition (including the concept of 'fundamentals') survive in his catholic
writing.[1]

It is true that Newman never sufficiently confronted the
problems posed by the fact that the content of the 'Episcopal
Tradition' is itself subject to significant historical change and
variation. Nevertheless, he did not make the mistake of with-
drawing the *magisterium* from the total process of tradition,
placing it outside the church in an effort to immunise its
pronouncements from problems of history and hermeneutic.
Indeed, where the relationship of episcopal (including papal)
authority to the life, thought and experience of the believing
community is concerned, far from accepting any non-
historical and naively abstract disjunction between the
ecclesia docens and the *ecclesia discens*,[2] Newman's mature
thought moved towards a profound appreciation of the complex tensions and interactions within the life of the church
which are essential if the process of tradition is to be faithful

to the word which it embodies. This emerges clearly from an examination of two of his late works: the *Letter to the Duke of Norfolk* and the preface to the 1877 edition of the *Via Media*.

No sooner had the Vatican Council ended, than the claim was made that only the strongest possible reading of the definition of papal primacy was compatible with catholic orthodoxy. Newman's friends begged him to publish something to restore the balance. The opportunity came when Gladstone, disturbed by the political implications of the definition, published a pamphlet entitled: *The Vatican Decrees in their Bearing on Civil Allegiance: A Political Expostulation*. 'According to Gladstone, papal infallibility meant that papal power was absolute since the pope himself could declare what was covered by *ex cathedra* decisions . . . Furthermore the claim to absolute and entire obedience to the pope at the peril of salvation in all matters of ecclesiastical discipline was not even qualified by a condition like *ex cathedra*' (Holmes [1969] pp 393–394). Newman answered Gladstone in the form of a long 'letter' to the young Duke of Norfolk (Diff II pp 171–378).

Although Newman rejected Gladstone's charge that the definition amounted to a '"repudiation of ancient history"' (Diff II p 308), he expressed 'the pleasure of heartily agreeing with him' when he insisted on 'the duty of "maintaining the truth and authority of history, and the inestimable value of the historic spirit"' (p 309). The issue is that of the relationship between history and religious belief, on which we touched in the previous chapter. In the *Letter*, Newman showed himself consistent with his earlier views in asserting that 'History never serves as the measure of dogmatic truth in its fullness' (p 206). 'For myself, I would simply confess that no doctrine of the Church can be rigorously proved by historical evidence; but at the same time that no doctrine can be simply disproved by it' (p 312; the whole passage is worth studying).

The other topic tackled in the *Letter* which is of particular interest to us is that of the relationship between the pronouncements of ecclesiastical authority and their reception by the believing community as a whole. Here Newman asserts a principle which, as we shall see, he was to develop more fully three years later: 'None but the *Schola Theologorum* is competent to determine the force of Synodal utterances, and the exact interpretation of them is a work of time' (p 176). He quotes from a letter which he had written six days after the promulgation of the definition: ' "if the definition is consistently received by the whole body of the faithful as valid, or as the expression of a truth, then too it will claim our assent by the force of the great dictum, *'Securus judicat orbis terrarum'*. This indeed is a broad principle by which all acts of the rulers of the Church are ratified" ' (p 303).

In the *Lectures on the Prophetical Office*, Newman had, as we have seen, levelled two charges against Roman catholicism: that it had illegitimately 'added' to the creed, and that it had allowed a gulf to develop between its theory and its practice. The *Essay on Development* was, in part, his answer to the first charge. He turned to the second in a long essay with which, in 1877, he prefaced the third edition of the *Via Media*. This important essay represents Newman's final view on the church. It 'directly influenced Von Hügel, whose celebrated analysis of religion into three elements in *The Mystical Element* is derived from Newman's preface' (Coulson [1967] p 124).[3]

The distinction between 'Prophetical' and 'Episcopal' tradition had been a distinction, not between a 'learning' and a 'teaching' church, but rather between the 'life' of the church and its 'form'. This distinction was now replaced by a 'threefold description of the Church as a community for teaching, worship and ministry' (Coulson [1970] p 173). The entire community of the church shares in the threefold office of Christ, as priest, prophet and king. These three offices Newman sees as being focussed, respectively, in the spiritual life of the local church, the scholarly community and the 'political' or ordering structure of government: 'Christianity, then, is at once a philosophy, a political power, and a religious rite . . . As a religion, its special centre of action is pastor and flock; as a philosophy, the Schools; as a rule, the Papacy and its Curia' (V.M. 1 p xl).

Each of these three aspects of the concrete reality of the church has its own proper structuring interest or concern. If any one of the three is allowed to flourish at the expense of the other two, the result will inevitably be a distortion of the church's experience, structure and activity. 'Truth is the guiding principle of theology and theological inquiries; devotion and edification, of worship; and of government, expedience. The instrument of theology is reasoning; of worship, our emotional nature; of rule, command and coercion. Further, in man as he is, reasoning tends to rationalism; devotion to superstition and enthusiasm; and power to ambition and tyranny' (p xli).

As a result, the concrete life of the church in history, the process of tradition, will only be healthy if these three functions are kept in balance, in a state of dynamic tension: 'Each of the three has its separate scope and direction; each has its own interests to promote and further; each has to find room for the claims of the other two; and each will find its own line of action influenced and modified by the others' (loc cit). Because the church is in business to hear and respond (in word and work) to the revelation of God, the word of life, 'Theology is the fundamental and regulating principle of the whole Church system . . . It is the subject-matter, the formal cause, the expression, of the Prophetical Office, and, as being such, has created both the Regal Office and the Sacerdotal. And it has in a certain sense a power of jurisdiction over those offices, as being its own creatures' (p xlvii).

I have dwelt at some length on this preface because it casts new light on the problem of assessing change, or development, in the church. I have insisted that, where problems of doctrinal change and continuity are concerned, the field of relevant data may not be restricted to the history of christian statements, but must include the whole range of the church's life and activity. The truth of christian 'theory' is too closely bound up with the quality of christian 'practice' for it to be possible to press the necessary distinction between 'theory' and 'practice' to the point where they can be handled as fundamentally separate issues. In 1837 Newman claimed that 'Action is the criterion of true faith' (V.M. 1 p 87). His principle that 'The safeguard of Faith is a right state of heart' (U.S. p 234) applies, not only to the individual, but to the church as a whole. In order to assess the 'truth', or faithfulness of a particular development of christian doctrine, it will be insufficient to ascertain that the development is a theoretically justifiable interpretation or application of new testament teaching. It will also be necessary to ask whether the development in question expresses or embodies a style of life, an ethical response, which is in conformity with the style of life commanded or recommended by the gospel.

To conclude this chapter, we can return to the problem of *magisterium*, and notice how closely a recent statement by one of Europe's most distinguished theologians echoes the patterns of Newman's preface to the *Via Media*. 'It is clear that the bishop, the theologian and the pastoral specialist have to work together, each according to his competence and capacities. It is Fr Schillebeeckx who once wrote that the tragedy of the modern Church resides in the fact that the three most important functions in the Church, the government, the theological reflection and the pastoral research have been merged into one competence, mostly that of the bishop. But their collaboration entails, because of the very nature of the Church as a communion, that the three of them are prepared to listen to what the Spirit is prompting in the People of God, to the "sensus fidei" of the whole Body' (Fransen [1972] pp 36–37).

NOTES

1. There is, I believe, ample evidence for this, although to provide such evidence is not possible in a general survey such as this. The clearest presentation of the opposite point of view is that found in Stern [1967].
2. The most recent study of the problem recognises this fact, but suffers from a tendency somewhat woodenly to impose a systematic theoretical structure on the subtle complexity of Newman's thought: cf Lease [1971].
3. The preface has recently received the detailed examination which it deserves: see Bergeron [1971].

11

MODERNISM: LITTLE RED BOOKS

According to one recent contributor to the history of modernism, 'the primary problem at issue was . . . that of justifying to oneself and for one's contemporaries structural Christianity in general, and structural Roman Catholic Christianity in particular' (Barmann [1972] pp x–xi). What had made this justification so urgently necessary was that complex of factors which went to make up the cultural revolution of the nineteenth century. Two of these factors, especially, are central to the themes with which we are concerned in this book. On the one hand, the irrevocable acquisition of a genuinely historical sense, generating the realisation that no human statement, no human institution, is 'absolute' in the sense that it can claim immunity from the particularity, the contingency, of the historical. On the other hand, the methodological revolution which made human experience the inevitable starting-point from which that enquiry is obliged to proceed, 'in concrete matters', by empirical techniques of argument and verification.

'The dogmas the Church holds out as revealed are not truths which have fallen from heaven. They are an interpretation of religious facts which the human mind has acquired by laborious effort' (Decree *Lamentabili Sane Exitu* prop 22; Denzinger 2022, quoted Reardon [1970] p 244). In this condemned proposition one can recognise, once again, that the root problem underlying any discussion of doctrinal change and continuity is the problem of revelation. Throughout the modernist debates, frequent references were made to 'hegelianism'. But if there is one nineteenth-century thinker whose questions (often unrecognised) lie at the heart of those debates, it is perhaps not Hegel, but rather Feuerbach.

In this chapter I propose to concentrate on Loisy's three 'little red books', because of their subsequent influence on catholic discussion of doctrinal development. The problem of the extent to which the conception of dogmatic statements argued for by some of the leading modernists, and especially by Tyrrell and Le Roy, leads to that agnosticism which Pius x, in the encyclical *Pascendi*, saw as its inevitable consequence, thus lies outside the scope of this chapter. But, because we shall have to return to this question later on, a brief comment on it is in order before turning to Loisy.

Newman once remarked: 'That a thing is true is no reason that it should be said, but that it should be done' (P.S. v p 45). The modernists recovered a sense of the existential, confessional nature of doctrinal statements. In contrast to the intellectualism which prevailed in the catholic theology of the period, they were deeply conscious that God's truth is saving truth: that God's self-disclosure in history invites man's response in deeds, and not merely in words.

At the same time, their profound sense of the inadequacy of all theological statements in respect of their object tended to be pressed to the point at which it becomes problematic whether what is affirmed in religious symbols can in any sense be said to be true or false as a statement about the mystery to which the symbol points. Nevertheless, the following characteristic statements by Le Roy would seem to be, at worst, infelicitous expressions of an important truth: 'First of all . . . a dogma has a *negative* meaning. It excludes and condemns certain errors, instead of positively determining the truth' (Le Roy [1918] p 57). 'From the strictly intellectual point of view it seems to me that dogmas have only the negative and prohibitive sense of which I speak. If they formulated absolute truth in adequate terms (to assume that such a fiction has a meaning) they would be unintelligible to us' (p 66).

In the winter of 1899–1900, Harnack delivered in Berlin a series of lectures on the essence of christianity which have been variously described as 'a distillate of the historical knowledge that already filled so many thousands of pages of his works' (Pelikan [1971] p 64), and as 'the highest expression and perfect manifestation of the age of bourgeois idealism' (Zahrnt [1969] p 15). The first world war dealt a death-blow to that idealism, and to the liberal protestantism which was its theological expression. But, although it may be easy, today, to indicate the weaknesses in Harnack's interpretative presuppositions, it is not difficult to see why, in their published form (*Das Wesen des Christentums*, Leipzig 1900; Eng trans Harnack [1901]), these lectures had so profound an impact, and such an enduring influence.

Harnack believed that it was possible for the historian, as historian, to isolate the 'essence' or 'kernel' of christianity from the 'husks' of its successive acculturations in doctrinal, liturgical and institutional forms. Jesus' teaching 'may be grasped under three heads. They are each of such a nature as to contain the whole . . . Firstly, the kingdom of God and its coming. Secondly, God the Father and the infinite value of the human soul. Thirdly, the higher righteousness and the commandment of love' (Harnack [1901] p 51). Even the first of these he interpreted in radically individualistic terms: 'it is the individual, not the nation or the state, which is redeemed' (p 60). Although he acknowledged that 'the Gospel aims at founding a community of men as wide as human life itself, and as deep as human need' (p 100), he believed that the process of redemption occurs solely through the transformation of individual consciousness, and not through the transformation of social and political structures.

He was too great an historian not to appreciate that the gospel cannot live, in history, without some embodiment in social and cultural forms: 'no religious movement can remain in a *bodiless* condition. It must elaborate *forms* for common life and common public worship' (p 181). But these forms remain, at best, the disposable 'husk', carrying and protecting the 'kernel' of the pure gospel. They have, for Harnack, a merely social or historical function: they are not forms of christian truth. At worst, 'the value of that to which [these forms] minister is insensibly transferred to them' (loc cit), and then they obscure, and threaten to destroy, the message they carry.

His particular interest, of course, was in that first great cultural shift in the history of the church: the hellenisation of christianity. Apologetically, the crucial question is: 'did the Gospel hold its own amid this change?' (p 197). One thing at least is clear: 'the whole outward and visible institution of a Church claiming divine dignity has no foundation whatever

in the Gospel. It is a case, not of distortion, but of total perversion' (p 262). Nevertheless, leading up to his triumphal
peroration on behalf of German protestantism, he is able to
answer his question in the affirmative: 'the power of the
Gospel . . . in spite of the frightful weight that it has to
carry, makes its way again and again' (pp 266–267).

The challenge was taken up by one of the most brilliant
French catholic scholars of the period, Alfred Loisy. When
L'Evangile et l'Eglise (Loisy [1902]) first appeared, it was
hailed as a first-rate piece of apologetic. Von Hügel called it
'"quite simply superb"' (quoted Heaney [1968] p 64);
Archbishop Mignot 'told Loisy that he felt this to be the most
comprehensive and objective thing that the latter had yet
written' (Barmann [1972] p 94); articles in the *Tablet* and
the *Month* praised it, as did Dom Cuthbert Butler and Wilfrid
Ward (cf Ward [1937] p 162). Most ironical of all: Cardinal
Sarto 'expressed great satisfaction with it with the exception
of certain passages he found obscure' (loc cit). Within a few
months, Cardinal Sarto was to become Pope Pius x.

The storm broke the following year, when Loisy published
the second 'little red book' (Loisy [1903]), a commentary—
in the form of letters—on *L'Evangile et l'Eglise*. It may have
been its 'heavily sarcastic' tone which was 'the real reason
behind the eventual rejection of the book by the Roman
authorities' (Barmann [1972] p 105). An equally plausible
explanation is to be found in the fact that, in the preface, he
spelt out the methodological principles with which he had
been working in the first book. The shock experienced by
those who had not previously grasped the implications of
L'Evangile et L'Eglise may account for the myth of Loisy's
duplicity. Thus Maisie Ward refers to the first book as 'a
gigantic and most successful hoax' (Ward [1937] p 162). In
fact, there is no doubt but that, when he published it, 'he was
sincerely Catholic. This was not to say that in *L'Evangile et
l'Eglise* he unfolded all that was in his mind' (Vidler [1970]
p 40).

The immediate reaction to the second book was the pro-
duction of a crop of articles insisting on the immutability of
dogma. Very soon, calmer and more thoughtful responses
began to appear (including the articles by Blondel which we

shall discuss in the following chapter), and 'la théologie de la tradition commence à être introduite franchement, dès cette époque, sous le signe de l'idée du développement' (da Veiga Coutinho [1954] pp 161–162). But an articulate challenge to presuppositions deeply held by those who occupy positions of power and responsibility is rarely exorcised by argument. 1907 saw the promulgation of the decree *Lamentabili*, and the encyclical *Pascendi*. It is perhaps not surprising that Loisy's analysis, in the third 'little red book' (Loisy [1908]), of the sixty-five propositions condemned in *Lamentabili* should be sometimes bitter and always sad. In the years that followed, as Pius x's reign of terror moved to its climax, 'The authorities destroyed a whole generation of thinkers within the Roman Catholic church, forcing those who would survive as members of that institution back into the thought patterns and formulae of another age' (Barmann [1972] p 245).

All the elements of *L'Evangile et l'Eglise* can be found in the series of six articles which he published in the *Revue du Clergé Francais* between December 1898 and October 1900.[1] In 1896 Loisy, who had read nothing of Newman's except '"des extraits d'un livre sur le développement doctrinal"' (quoted Vidler [1934] p 93), asked Von Hügel which of the cardinal's works he would recommend. It was presumably then that Von Hügel sent him a copy of the *Essay on Development* of which, as we have already noticed, the first of the six articles was a lucid and enthusiastic summary and critique. In it he distinguished three 'moments' in the process of development: the 'real', the 'theological' and the 'dogmatic'. Of the first, he said: 'Au fond il y a autre chose et beaucoup plus qu'un mouvement d'idées; il y a toute la vie de l'Eglise. Newman l'a mieux vu et mieux dit que personne avant lui' (Loisy [1898] p 14). The main purpose of all six articles is to mount a critique of Harnack's *History of Dogma* and, especially, of Auguste Sabatier's *Esquisse d'une Philosophie de la Religion*. At the end of this first article, he wrote: '*L'Histoire des dogmes* de M. Harnack est plus érudite que *L'Essai sur le développement de la doctrine chrétienne*; mais combien elle lui est inférieure pour l'intelligence générale du christianisme et de sa vie multiple, du rapport intime qui existe entre toutes les formes et toutes les phases de cette vie' (p 20).

At this stage, Loisy's view of the indispensability, and yet inevitable inadequacy of dogmatic statements, and of their constant need of restatement, 'completion' and 'explanation' is very close to Newman's (cf Loisy [1899a] p 213). Sabatier had denied that revelation is '"une communication une fois faite de doctrines immuables et qu'il n'y aurait qu'à retenir"' (quoted Loisy [1900a] p 250). Catholic doctrine has never claimed this, answers Loisy. The notions of 'doctrines immuables' and 'retention' should be replaced by 'vérités certaines', and 'expliquer et développer' (loc cit). 'La révélation n'existe pas tant que la vérité révélée n'est pas devenu intelligible à l'homme et ne s'est pas comme réalisée en lui' (p 258).

Harnack had always insisted that he wrote as an historian. In *L'Evangile et l'Eglise*, therefore, Loisy asserts, at the outset, that he too is writing 'au point de vue de l'histoire' (Loisy [1902] p vii). No other course was open to him, if his critique of Harnack was to be apologetically effective. But although the methodological distinction between the task of the historian and that of the theologian is sharply made, he insists that 'Un incompatibilité radicale n'existe pas entre la profession de théologien et celle de l'historien' (pp x–xi).

According to Harnack, the essence of christianity had been obscured, and sometimes corrupted, by the social and cultural forms through which it had passed. Loisy's technique is to reply: no, not corrupted; in each new linguistic, cultural or political context, this or that development of christianity had been 'necessary'. But what does 'necessary' mean, in this connection? The argument is not lacking in ambiguity, but it would seem that, fundamentally, Loisy was no more endorsing a theory of historical determinism than Newman had been when, in the *Essay on Development*, he had employed a similar argument for a similarly apologetic purpose. Loisy's argument is that, from the historian's point of view, many of the changes which took place would seem to have been unavoidable, if the reality of christianity was to survive. The weakness of this approach, as Tyrrell recognised, was that '"it does not give us what Newman tried (vainly I think) to give us, a criterion to distinguish true from false developments"' (quoted Vidler [1934] p 165). Nevertheless, Loisy did occasionally provide hints of an approach to the problem of criteriology which was not to bear fruit for many decades: 'Ce qui est vraiment évangélique dans le christianisme d'aujourd'hui n'est pas ce qui n'a jamais changé, car, en un sens, tout a changé et n'a jamais cessé de changer; mais ce qui, nonobstant tous les changements extérieurs, procède de l'impulsion donnée par le Christ, s'inspire de son esprit, sert le même idéal et la même espérance' (Loisy [1902] pp 67–68).

Harnack had said that the church, as it appeared in history, was a corruption. No, replied Loisy. Once the expectation of an imminent parousia receded, the only way in which the message could have survived was through the emergence of the church. This is the context of the famous, and frequently misunderstood phrase: 'Jésus annoncait le royaume, et c'est l'Eglise qui est venue' (p 111).

Loisy, like Newman before him, frequently employs the analogy of literary criticism or interpretation to describe the relationship between the originating events and subsequent developments in the life of the church. Thus, in a passage which establishes the terms in which the debate will be conducted for the next fifty years: 'L'enseignement et l'apparition même de Jésus ont dû être interprétés. Toute la question est de savoir si le commentaire est homogène ou hétérogène au texte' (p 128; notice similar terminology in Loisy [1903] p 12).

It is not difficult to trace the source of the condemned proposition which we quoted at the beginning of this chapter: 'Les conceptions que l'Eglise présente comme des dogmes révélés ne sont pas des vérités tombées du ciel et gardées par la tradition religieuse dans la forme précise où ils ont paru d'abord. L'historien y voit l'interprétation de faits religieux, acquise par un laborieux effort de la pensée théologique' (Loisy [1902] p 159; cf Loisy [1908], where he refers to this passage, in a different edition of L'Evangile et l'Eglise). Loisy's own conception of the respective roles of divine activity and human experience in revelation, as stated in Autour d'un Petit Livre, is balanced and succinct: 'C'est l'homme qui cherche, mais c'est Dieu qui l'excite; c'est l'homme qui voit, mais c'est Dieu qui l'éclaire. La révélation se réalise dans l'homme, mais elle est l'oeuvre de Dieu en lui, avec lui et par lui' (Loisy [1903] p 198).

In the last resort, we do not do justice to either Harnack or Loisy if we see in the former the implacable foe, or in the latter the uncritical advocate, of all historical development. For Harnack, development, which is inevitable, only has value to the extent that it illuminates the central intuition of christianity. For Loisy, development is the progressive un- folding of the implications of an originally rich and complex reality (cf Poulat [1962] p 96). Neither of them captured the balance of Newman who, while he continually insisted that christian experience and understanding is focussed on, finds its centre in, the mystery of Christ, yet refused to opt for that reductionism which has been a recurring feature of the search for the 'essence' of christianity.

Loisy was fighting a battle on two fronts: on the one hand against Harnack's reductionism; on the other, on behalf of the legitimate methodological autonomy of the critical his- torian. *L'Evangile et l'Eglise* was an apologetic sketch, not a balanced treatise: 'C'est la notion même du développement qui a maintenant besoin de se développer, et l'on n'a pas à la créer de toutes pièces, mais à constituer d'après une meilleure connaissance du passé' (Loisy [1902] p 162). This lesson was only slowly, and painfully, to be learnt.

NOTES

1. Loisy [1898], [1899a], [1899b], [1900a], [1900b], [1900c]. An excellent summary of these articles may be found in Poulat [1962], pp 74–88.

12

BLONDEL: HISTORY AND DOGMA

In 1886, Maurice Blondel wrote: '"I propose to study action, because it seems to me that the Gospel attributes to action alone the power to manifest love and to attain God! Action is the abundance of the heart"' (quoted Dru, introduction to Blondel [1964] p 33). In 1893, he produced what was to remain (in spite of the enormous output of his later years) his most enduring philosophical work: *L'Action*. Blondel's epistemological stance has significant affinities with Newman's, and especially with the latter's lifelong preference for 'faith', as distinct from 'reason' (as these terms are defined and used in the *University Sermons*), as a means of attaining truth 'in concrete matters'. Blondel was a philosopher preoccupied all his life with showing that the human spirit is, in the concreteness of its knowing and loving and questioning, open to the mystery of God. In this chapter, we shall be discussing Blondel's contribution to his debate with Loisy. This was not simply a debate between an historian and a philosopher. Underlying the methodological gulf which separated them, there was a radical difference of epistemological attitudes.

In 1894, von Hügel published an article in the *Dublin Review* (von Hügel [1894]), which was 'a profound and moving plea to take the bible seriously as a *human* book so that it could achieve its maximum effectiveness as a vehicle for *divine* revelation' (Barmann [1972] p 51). Such a concern played an important part in Loisy's *L'Evangile et l'Eglise*. Yet it seemed to Blondel that, in his jealousy to preserve the historian's methodological autonomy lest too hasty claims by theology prove self-defeating by obscuring that human truth which was the form of divine truth's historical appearance, Loisy ran the risk of restricting historical truth to that which could be established by the methods of the critical historian. Blondel's criticism of Loisy is not unlike that with which Newman reacted to what he regarded as the reductionist tendencies in the work of the historian, Milman; a reaction which, as we saw in chapter 9, Newman summed up in his reminder that 'what is historically human may be doctrinally divine' (Ess II p 230).

In 1903, Percy Gardner, the editor of the *Hibbert Journal*, reviewing *L'Evangile et l'Eglise*, objected that Loisy 'had too much separated history and doctrine' (Barmann [1972] p 96). Barmann, endorsing von Hügel's defence of Loisy against Gardner and Blondel, says that 'Loisy's position was not that of either history or dogma, but of both history and dogma, though at different levels and with different methodologies to explicate them' (loc cit). But that hardly meets the charge of excessive separation.

Blondel's initial reaction to *L'Evangile et l'Eglise* was appreciative but, in the weeks that followed his first reading of it, his reservations increased and multiplied (cf Poulat [1962] p 516). At one point in the ensuing correspondence with Loisy, it seemed that they might reach agreement (p 529), but the gulf that separated them was too wide. In February 1903, in a letter to von Hügel, Blondel distinguished between '*l'évolution*, effet des pressions extérieures, et le *développement*, création continuée à partir d'un germe qui transsubstantie ses aliments. Le développement dont parle Loisy n'est en réalité qu'une évolution' (p 544). Eventually, Blondel decided to publish his criticisms, and in 1904 *History and Dogma* appeared, initially in the form of three articles.[1] He did not explicitly mention either Loisy or his book, because 'He had no wish to get Loisy into trouble with the authorities' (Dru; Blondel [1964] p 212). The disadvantage of this method, however, was that it absolved him from the need to discuss specific assertions by Loisy. Instead, he was able to contruct an 'ideal-type', to which, as we shall see, he gave the name of 'historicism' (cf Poulat [1970] p 544). This may have made for philosophical clarity, but it did not help the dialogue with Loisy.

'If Christian facts (history) and Christian beliefs (dogma) coincided in the light of immediate experience or complete evidence; if we only had to *believe* what others have *seen* and affirmed, the difficulty would not arise. But it is generally agreed that there is, as it were, a double movement between fact and faith, a sort of coming and going over two obscure intervals: for while it is true that historical facts are the foundations of the Catholic faith, they do not of themselves engender it, nor do they suffice to justify it entirely; and, reciprocally, the Catholic faith and the authority of the Church which it implies guarantee the facts and draw from them a doctrinal interpretation which convinces the believer as would a historical reality itself, but on other grounds than those which the historian is able to verify' (Blondel [1964] p 223). For example, Jesus claimed to be the messiah, and the early church affirmed that he was the Son of God. What is the process by which the move is made from the first affirmation to the second, and how is the second grounded in the first?

Having thus stated the problem as he sees it, Blondel then proceeds to describe and criticise 'two incomplete and incompatible solutions', which he calls 'extrinsicism' and 'historicism', while apologising for these 'barbarous neologisms' (pp 224, 225).

He deals with the first quite briefly, because his real interest is in Loisy, the proponent of 'historicism'. A certain type of catholic theology and apologetic has no interest in, or feel for, history as such. Historical facts, events or sayings are treated merely as pegs on which to hang timeless, unqualified, absolute truths. The link between these truths and the historical facts with which they are connected is merely 'extrinsic'. 'The Bible is guaranteed *en bloc* . . . the ageless facts are without local colour, vanish, as the result of a sort of perpetual docetism, into a light that casts no shadow, and disappear beneath the weight of the absolute by which they are crushed' (p 229). As more and more people came to see that such a method simply does not work, 'some who were firmly anchored in their well-founded faith remained systematically hostile to everything which contradicted not only *the* faith but *their* faith; whilst others drifted haphazardly without knowing whether it was towards harbour or shipwreck, almost equally scandalised by the blindness of those who close their eyes to the facts, and by the importunate curiosity and the disturbing affirmations of those who expect too much light from them' (p 231).

Loisy had insisted that history and theology are distinct disciplines, and had pleaded for the autonomy of historical method. Blondel, early in his analysis of 'historicism', the other 'incomplete solution', asks: 'in what sense can one say that history is independent?' (p 234). If history is distinguished from theology on the basis of their 'objects' (in the sense of what scholastic terminology would have referred to as 'material objects'), then 'the historian purely as such performs his task behind his partition; he carries out his researches from his own point of view; and his labour finally furnishes a slice of real life and of absolute truth. Others must put up as best they can with his conclusions, which are what they are: so much the worse if they contradict other conclusions' (p 235).

However, according to 'The more recent conception of science and the sciences . . . these sciences differ . . . less in respect of the diversity of their objects . . . than in the diversity of methods and points of view opening on to an ulterior problem which they collaborate to define . . . while the historian has, as it were, a word to say in everything concerning man, there is nothing on which he has the last word' (pp 235–236).

The methodological gulf separating Loisy from Blondel is so wide that it is difficult to assess the extent to which Blondel's analysis of the implications of Loisy's method does justice to the latter. Be that as it may, the importance of this section of *History and Dogma* lies in Blondel's insistence that, while history and theology are distinct in the abstract, in the concrete they converge in virtue of the fact that men who are at once historians and believers attempt coherently to relate to their past. And the relationship between the concrete subject and his past is not simply historical (in the sense that the past only exists in so far as it may be susceptible of critical historical proof), but is also theological (in the sense that certain events in the past have a religious, an existential value for us, and not merely an historical value). By 'historicism', Blondel means the habit of erroneously confusing that living history which is our total, complex, concrete relationship to our past, with that abstract, scientific history which is, in fact, simply one (indispensable) way of approaching, or reflecting on, the total reality. 'The danger to which I am calling attention under the name of "*historicism*" lies in the alternative between "real history" and "scientific history" or the substitution of one for the other' (p 239).

Loisy, in his defence of catholicism against Harnack, had tended to describe the successive developments of doctrine, practice and structure as historically 'necessary' or 'inevitable'. 'Historicism', according to Blondel, thus 'tends to look for the whole subject-matter of history in the *evolution* which unfolds the series of events under the pressure of the forces which compose our world, and for its form in the mechanical explanation of that kaleidoscope' (p 241). In terms of the historiographical debates of our own day, Blondel is accusing Loisy of acknowledging only the 'external' history of doctrine, to the neglect of its 'internal' history.[2]

Returning to his initial account of the 'double movement between fact and faith', Blondel insists that, since we cannot accept either the obliteration of the historical by dogmatic certainty, nor rest content with recognising the methodological differences between history and theology, it must be possible to give some intelligible account of the relationship between the christian facts and the christian ideas: 'on the one hand, the facts exist for the sake of the ideas; on the other, the ideas exist for the sake of the facts, for the *acts*, and gravitate around them' (p 252). In the final part of his study, he tries to meet this need by arguing for a particular conception of 'tradition'.

The notion of tradition has been neglected in recent decades, he says, because 'The usual idea evoked by the word Tradition is that of a transmission, principally by word of mouth, of historical facts, received truths, accepted teachings' (p 265). But is this, 'where Catholicism is concerned, the essential content of the notion?' (loc cit). The alternative conception which he puts forward is already familiar to us because, through the work of Congar, especially, it has—at least in its broad outlines—become a commonplace of catholic theology. Tradition is the total process of the historical life of a society: 'it preserves not so much the intellectual aspect of the past as its living reality' (p 267). '"To keep" the word of God means in the first place to do it, to put it into practice; and the deposit of Tradition . . . cannot be transmitted in its entirety, indeed, cannot be used and developed, unless it is confided to the practical obedience of love' (p 274). Not only is this passage strikingly reminiscent of Newman but, through it, one can detect the outlines of the characteristically Blondelian concept of 'action'.

The closing pages of *History and Dogma* undoubtedly constituted a breakthrough in the theology of tradition. And yet, Blondel has little to offer us directly where problems of authority, of criteriology, are concerned: 'As against those who offer us a Christianity so divine that there is nothing human, living or moving about it, and those who involve it so deeply in historical contingencies and make it so dependent upon natural factors that it retains nothing but a diffused divinity, we must show it to be both more concrete and more universal, more divine and more human, than words can express' (p 286).

No sooner had Blondel's articles appeared than Louis Venards jumped to Loisy's defence, in an article which distorted Blondel's argument by oversimplifying it (Venards [1904]). In particular, Venards transformed Blondel's distinction between the 'historical value' and the 'religious value' of the past from a distinction of aspects into a distinction between separate orders of reality, only connected 'par une sorte d'intuition' (Venards [1904] p 347). He also charged Blondel with holding that the 'religious value' of a fact 'garantit sa valeur historique' (p 352).

Blondel was thus provided with an opportunity of showing, at some length, that the heart of the matter lay in the ambiguity of the concept of an 'historical fact': 'Le mot *fait*, qu'on emploie couramment comme s'il était univoque, a de multiples acceptions' (Blondel [1956] p 237; first published 1905). The following month, we find von Hügel writing to Blondel: '"while it is impossible for *all* the 'facts' of Christianity not at all to be also facts of a full and ordinary historicity, *one or another*, may in time *be discovered to be, not less true than formerly but of another type of truth*"' (quoted Heaney [1968] p 106). And, many years later, Venards wrote: '"sur les rapports du dogme et de l'histoire, je ne crois pas que rien n'ait été écrit de plus éclairant que les articles de Blondel dans *La Quinzaine* et sa réponse au *Bulletin de Littérature Ecclésiastique*"' (quoted Poulat [1962] p 605).

It is not unknown for historians of the modernist crisis to criticise Blondel for failing to do justice to Loisy. Thus, for example, according to Barmann, 'Blondel and his sympathisers really did fail to understand historical method, both in its manner of proceeding and in the objects of its research' (Barmann [1972] p 122). But to defend Loisy by indicating Blondel's weaknesses is no more helpful than the reverse procedure which, in the same passage, Barmann rightly criticises. In the last resort, to ask which man was 'right' is to trivialise the debate. Both men were attempting to tackle, from very different methodological and temperamental standpoints, fundamental problems concerning the historicity of christian truth. Since 1905, developments in historiography, hermeneutics and the methodology of the social sciences have forced both historians and theologians to reconsider certain of the presuppositions with which Loisy and Blondel worked. The debate between them can nevertheless still cast light on the problems with which they were mutually concerned. It is only in very recent years that catholic theology has begun to take with full seriousness those questions of historical epistemology towards which Blondel's reply to Venards, especially, was beginning to point (cf Poulat [1970] pp 535–536).

NOTES

1. Maurice Blondel, 'Histoire et Dogme. Les Lacunes Philosophiques de l'Exégèse Moderne'. *La Quinzaine*, lvi (1904) pp 145–167, 349–373, 433–458. References are to the English edition, published in Blondel [1964].
2. For a subtle application of this distinction to related problems in the history and philosophy of science, see Hesse [1970].

13

HOMOGENEOUS EVOLUTION

Discussion of 'progress' in christian theology, of the process whereby revealed truth is more clearly explained or logically unfolded, was by no means unknown before the nineteenth century (cf Chadwick [1957] pp 74–95). But the historical frame of reference within which this earlier discussion took place was fundamentally static. 'To the scientists and philosophers of Butler's world, nature seemed like a beautifully designed and arranged mechanism. The scientists and philosophers of the 1840s were beginning to see nature as an organism, were beginning to use words like "development" or "evolution" to describe her processes' (p 95). It was thus inevitable that older explanations of doctrinal change and variation should begin 'to break down before the new historical sense of the nineteenth century' (p 193).

In the previous three chapters, we have seen some of the ways in which this 'new historical sense' found expression in different responses to the problem of the historicity of christian truth. The first Vatican Council affirmed the permanence of the meaning of dogmatic statements; the official reaction to the modernists asserted the immutability of dogma in uncompromising terms; Newman sought for a 'view' of christian history such that, in the shifting kaleidoscope of historical process, the essential continuity and maintained identity of the christian 'idea' could be discerned; Harnack envisaged that history as the heroic, and ultimately successful, struggle of the 'essence' of christianity to withstand the corrupting influence of successive cultural contexts; Loisy regarded those successive contexts as the necessary forms of the gospel in history; Blondel recognised the need for a concept of 'tradition' in which the ongoing life and obedience of the community were indispensable for the discovery and transmission of christian truth.

Both Newman and Blondel recognised that the challenge

which the church began to experience during the nineteenth century was not exclusively, or even primarily, a challenge to faith or to theology. It was the religious dimension of a deeper cultural revolution. Therefore any adequate response to it had to take place at all the levels, theoretical, devotional and institutional, at which men attempt to respond to a deepening awareness of their own historicity. The experience of the erosion of absolutes is by no means restricted to christian believers. 'The crisis' in which we are involved, says Bernard Lonergan, 'is a crisis not of faith but of culture' (Lonergan [1967a] p 266).

Similarly, both Newman and Blondel appreciated that the range of data relevant to an examination of doctrinal change and continuity is as wide as the entire life, structure, thought and activity of the christian community.

One tragic consequence of the Roman catholic church's negative response to the challenge, in suppressing the modernists, was that, for about forty years (from 1910 to 1950), catholic theology was forced to operate within a hopelessly restricted frame of reference. Sooner or later, another explosion was (as Loisy might have said) 'inevitable'. It is with the main tendencies in catholic discussion of problems of doctrinal development, during those forty years, that we are concerned in this chapter.

In the aftermath of the modernist crisis, catholic thinking was inhibited by an inter-related set of deep-seated fears: fear of discussion of 'change' or 'evolution'; fear of any appeal to 'experience', or 'feeling', or 'the religious sense'; and a fear of the possible results of historical and exegetical enquiry. As a result, most of the writing during this period was marked by a twofold emphasis: on the immutability and objectivity of doctrinal statements, and on the teaching authority (*magisterium*) of those in official positions (the *Magisterium*). To this twofold emphasis there correspond the two broad groups into which it is convenient to classify modern catholic theories of doctrinal development: 'logical' and 'theological'. Before considering these two types, it is necessary to say something about the concept which, for four decades, provided the framework for the discussion: the concept of 'homogeneous evolution'.

Herbert Spencer's conception of 'progress' as 'an advance from homogeneity of structure to heterogeneity of structure' (Spencer [1966] p 154), was partly influenced by Coleridge. It represents a line of thought completely different from that which found expression in the use made of the terms 'homogeneous' and 'heterogeneous' in twentieth-century catholic theology. The temptation to confuse them may be due to the persistent attempts to father theories of 'homogeneous evolution' on Newman, who was influenced by Coleridge,[1] although there is no evidence that he was influenced by Spencer. We have already seen, in chapter 9, that such attempts tend rather to mislead than to clarify. One of the very few passages in which Newman used the term 'homogeneous' in a sense similar to that which it acquired in the period with which we are concerned occurs in the *Apologia*: 'The new truth which is promulgated, if it is to be called new, must be at least homogeneous, cognate, implicit, viewed relatively to the old truth' (Apo p 253).

According to Loisy, Harnack had maintained that 'le fait ecclésiastique est comme étranger, hétérogène, adventice au fait évangélique', whereas he himself 'a vouloue montrer que les deux faits sont connexes, homogènes, intimement liés, ou plutôt qu'ils sont le même fait dans son unité durable'.[2] Paradoxically, it is Loisy who here clearly formulates that statement of the problem which was to become classical in 'respectable' catholic theology. The appeal to 'homogeneity' is defensive. It amounts to a rejection of any claim that christian belief and doctrine, however varied the range of cultural contexts in which they have lived, have ever undergone a *metabasis eis allo genos*. The conception of christian history which it opposed was therefore described as 'transformist'.[3]

The notion of 'homogeneous evolution' eventually came to mark the limits within which (so it was supposed) any orthodox discussion of doctrinal development must take place. This was in no small measure due to the massive influence of Marin-Sola's study (to which we shall return). Marin-Sola, in common with all those who took part in the debate between the two world wars, simply took for granted that, once the fact of historical process had been (albeit reluctantly) admitted, then the best model by means of which to describe

this process was that of 'evolution'. Similarly, at least since
the publication of Newman's *Essay*, it has been assumed that
the process is appropriately described by the term 'development'. We shall have occasion to question these assumptions
in a later chapter. For the time being it is sufficient to notice
that the often brilliant and subtle theories which were con-
structed were rarely tested—with any seriousness—against
the complex historical data which they purported to interpret. To argue, on the basis of various cultural and doctrinal presuppositions, that the history of christian doctrine
'must be' a process of 'homogeneous evolution' is not necessarily to establish that this has, in fact, been the case.

Even in a cultural context in which it was simply assumed,
on all sides, that the process of history was to be conceived of
as a process of 'evolution', 'development' or 'progress', the
concept of 'homogeneous evolution' was, at best, imprecise,
and, at worst, dangerously misleading. It was sometimes used
simply as one expression of the christian trust that the gospel
proclaimed in the doctrine and life of the church is not *another* message from that proclaimed by the apostles. But,
secondly, this antecedent trust was sometimes so extended as
to amount to a denial, before any examination of the evidence, that any significant change or reorientation had taken
place in the belief, doctrine or practice of the church. (In this
form, it was closely connected with the tendency, during the
first half of the century, to extend almost indefinitely the
range of applicability of the concept of infallibility). Thirdly,
it sometimes expressed a mental attitude towards the history
of revelation, the process of tradition, which saw that process
as being virtually independent of, or only extrinsically related to, the general social, cultural and political history of
which it forms a part. (In this form, it was closely connected
with a set of attitudes towards the relationship between
'nature' and 'grace', 'reason' and 'revelation', which can
hardly be said to take with full seriousness the implications
of the doctrine of the incarnation).

In view of the fact that they were born of a defensive, and
largely negative reaction to the modernist crisis, and reared in
a climate heavy with suspicion of contemporary scholarship
and social change, theories of 'homogeneous evolution' para-

doxically bear witness to the very phenomenon they were elaborated to deny: namely, the culturally and historically conditioned nature of successive contexts of christian thought and expression.

Any classification of theories of doctrinal development is bound to be somewhat arbitrary. For the sake of convenience, however, I shall accept the standard distinction between 'logical' and 'theological' theories. 'A theory of development is called "logical" because according to it the process of development is simply described in terms of logical inference and the criterion of its truth is the logical test, whereas the qualification *theological* means that the process is conceived of as partaking of the character of mystery that is proper to the object of theology, and that the criterion of its truth does not properly consist in a logical verification but in a charismatic decision accepted by faith' (Walgrave [1972] p 165).

'Logical' theories represented an attempt to transpose the late scholastic problem of the definability of theological conclusions into a theory of doctrinal development (cf Hammans [1967] p 53). The most distinguished attempt in this direction was that made by Marin-Sola, whose study Chadwick described as 'perhaps the most influential thesis upon the theory of development written during the twentieth century' (Chadwick [1957] p 204). Marin-Sola's achievement was considerable and courageous. Nevertheless, in order to show the straits to which the anti-modernist reaction had reduced catholic studies of the problem, it is only necessary to consider a few characteristic features of the book.

In the first place, his concept of revelation is resolutely propositional. God reveals words with meanings which are, as it were, inserted into history by being supernaturally communicated to the apostles. The process of dogmatic development is that by which the church renders explicit the implicit aspects of the meaning of the statements of the apostles.

In the second place, 'the church', in Marin-Sola's usage, refers too often only to the hierarchy. We are told that 'the church', in its definitions, is not bound either by the arguments of theologians, or by the opinions of the faithful, for it is not the pupil, but the teacher of both (cf Marin-Sola [1924] i p 358).

Marin-Sola had a high regard for Newman's *Essay*, which he referred to as that 'immortal work' (i p 352). But the neo-scholastic frame of reference within which Marin-Sola operated was so narrow that he decided, albeit with apparent reluctance, that the *Essay* lays too much stress on life, on experience, on practice, as means by which catholic dogma develops (i p 351).

In the fourth place, the extension of the range of applicability of the description '*de fide*' has now reached the point where Marin-Sola can argue that any truly theological conclusion, admitted as certain by the general consensus of theologians, is patent of infallible definition as a doctrine to be held by divine faith (ii p 63).

The strength of 'logical' theories of development is their preoccupation with that element of rationality which must form part of any convincing claim that doctrine articulated at one period of christian history is a 'development' of earlier doctrine. The strength of the 'theological' theories, on the other hand, lies in their emphasis on the unpredictability of historical process, and on the fact that, theologically, the ultimate ground of doctrinal development is the Spirit of God, and not merely the mind of man.

This second group of theories tended to stress the uniqueness of the process of tradition. Thus Walgrave, who firmly endorses the 'theological' type of approach, says that 'Cultural tradition as far as it is merely cultural . . . has grown out of the common human experience and its interpretation by the intellect, whereas the Christian tradition proceeds from a special revelation connected with definite historical facts and an original interpretation whose truth is divinely guaranteed' (Walgrave [1972] pp 377–378). But what is the force of that 'whereas'? Such a passage suggests that some exceedingly difficult questions concerning the nature of revelation, the nature of historical facticity, and the role of 'common human experience and its interpretation by the intellect' in even a 'divinely guaranteed' interpretation, are being handled with a confidence which, in the present state of theology and hermeneutics, may reasonably be regarded as improvident.

One danger of the stress on the uniqueness of the process of christian tradition, and on the extent to which this process is not subject to the 'laws of history', is the emphasis that it necessarily places on the authoritative function of popes or councils. A strong doctrine of infallibility, together with a theology of *magisterium* which restricts the function of teachership in the church to a small group of individuals, easily combine to produce a state of affairs in which it is claimed that, 'in principle, and not only in fact, a theologian can perceive a truth as coming from revelation only in the light of the magisterium' (Hammans [1967] p 60). Hammans correctly describes such a position as 'theological agnosticism'.[4]

It is important to remember that this second group of theories of development flourished in the context of preparation for the definition of the dogma of the assumption. Here, if ever there was, was a doctrine which could not be rigorously deduced from biblical propositions.

Both before and after the definition, attention was increasingly paid to the *sensus fidei* as a factor in the process of tradition. Of itself, this was a healthy development, in that it marked an escape from the excessively intellectualist straitjacket into which 'logical' theories of development had enclosed the problem. It also represented a stage in the recovery of the ancient truth that the *whole* church in its life, belief and piety, is the 'carrier' of tradition, in which the shared 'sense of faith' gives rise to the *consensus fidelium*.

But, as a criteriological principle, an appeal to the *consensus fidelium* is notoriously fragile, especially when such an appeal is made only when more favoured sources of verification—exegetical and historical—have failed. Is not the 'religious sense' of the christian people the product and expression of many factors other than the gospel of Jesus Christ? One of the many areas in which we have lost our innocence is that of the sociology of knowledge! Moreover, in making an appeal to the '"religious sense with which the Christian people are imbued"' (Pius XII, *Ad Caeli Reginam*, quoted Hammans [1967] p 63), is not the *magisterium* itself subject to the same cultural, theological and spiritual limitations as the people whose 'religious sense' it claims to interpret and assess?

Karl Rahner quotes Friedrich Heiler as saying that the dogma of 1950 seems to be the proof that the modernist interpretation was, with one blow, taken up and even exceeded by Roman catholic apologists (cf Rahner [1969] p 320). No catholic is likely to be entirely happy with that forceful way of putting the objection. But it does seem to be the case that there are disturbing similarities between the thorough-going evolutionism of some of the modernists, for whom the new testament was only of interest as the 'germ' from which the great 'tree' of catholic theory and practice had grown, and theories of doctrinal development which attach, in practice, exclusive normative significance to contemporary christian experience and its interpretation by ecclesiastical authority. It is not, I think, entirely fanciful to suggest that, from some points of view, there is more in common between modernism, and the official thinking which so violently rejected it, than either party could possibly have appreciated at the time.[5] So long as theology continues to attribute unique normative significance, in principle, to the apostolic witness to Christ, then a tension between past and present should be a constitutive feature of christian hermeneutics. In much official theology, during the period we are considering, that tension was dangerously relaxed in favour of the present.

As recently as 1968, a standard reference work of catholic theology claimed that 'Once the dogma has evolved, the task theology has of showing its homogeneity with the deposit will sometimes be a difficult and delicate one' (Pozo [1968] p 101). In view of the defensive climate in which modern theories of doctrinal development were originally elaborated, it is not surprising that they should have been conceived as fulfilling a primarily justificatory role. But apologetics is hardly the basic function of theological enquiry, especially where historical investigation is concerned. Almost without exception, studies of doctrinal development produced between 1910 and 1950 were speculative, apologetic, theoretical exercises, which paid little attention to the complex historical data. Apologetics is more likely to engender false consciousness than it is historical understanding. The development of catholic biblical and historical studies eventually gave rise, especially in France, to a more empirical, less apologetically orientated, historical theology. To this recovery of history we must now turn.

NOTES

1. For the best discussion of the nature and extent of this influence, see Coulson [1970].
2. Loisy [1903] p 12. Walgrave, who is determined to classify Loisy amongst the proponents of 'transformistic' theories of development, claims that, according to the latter, 'transformative adaptation is the very law of history' (Walgrave [1972] p 247).
3. Walgrave casts his net so wide that Hegel, Schleiermacher, Loisy, Bultmann and Van Buren can all be offered as proponents of 'transformistic' theories: cf Walgrave [1972] pp 179–277.
4. Hammans [1967] p 60. We have already seen, in Chapter 10, that, in common with other proponents of 'theological' theories of development, Walgrave tends to make the teaching authority *external* to the community of the church. My references in this chapter to Walgrave's study are not, I think, inappropriate, even though we are concerned with the state of affairs which obtained between 1910 and 1950 because, from some points of view, Walgrave still works within the framework of the earlier debate.
5. This is a point which Karl Barth was fond of making: cf eg his discussion of 'the grandiose loneliness of the Church of the present' in Barth [1936] p 297.

14

THE RECOVERY OF HISTORY

The end of the second world war saw a considerable theological revival, especially in France. One of the distinctive features of what was called, at the time, 'la nouvelle théologie', was its sensitivity to historical problems. Throughout this book, I have set questions of theological and dogmatic development in the broader context of discussion of revelation, tradition and doctrine. It was this broader context from which the specific problem of 'dogmatic development' emerged in the nineteenth century, and to which it has returned in the twentieth. In France, the 'more limited debate about the development of dogma was . . . quickly eclipsed by the fundamental discussion about the concepts of faith in which the whole of the "new" theology was involved' (Schoof [1970] p 203). The status of the concepts of faith that were currently used in the church formed the centre of this wider debate. 'As a result of historical studies, questions were asked about the identity of these concepts with the authentic gospel of Christ and, thanks to an increasing awareness of the fact that man's thinking was closely interwoven with the progress of history and society, doubt was cast on their value as an interpretation of modern Christian experience' (p 201).

Although the 'new theology' did not produce any major work on doctrinal development, de Lubac, one of its chief protagonists, did publish in 1948 an article of considerable interest (de Lubac [1948]). De Lubac's article was occasioned by an article of Boyer's, which had appeared in 1940 (Boyer [1940]), but which remained unknown to de Lubac until after the war.

De Lubac criticised Boyer for trying to drag the problem back to where it had been during the period in which the least plausible theories of the 'logical' type had flourished, by reducing the vast and complex problem of change and development to the question of the definability of theological

conclusions (cf de Lubac [1948] p 131). Since then, the debate
had moved on, and, under the influence of the more creative
aspects of Marin-Sola's study, the increasing emphasis laid
on the 'consciousness of the church' as a factor in doctrinal
development had helped to widen the discussion.

Where Boyer only seemed able to see a process of linear
development, by way of rigorous deductive logic, de Lubac
insisted that 'la réalité nous montre une réaction perpétuelle
aux données ambiantes, par voie de défense, d'élimination,
de triage, de transformation, d'assimilation' (p 139).

De Lubac acknowledged that Boyer had located a crucial
weakness in 'theological' theories of development. 'Comment pourrait-on dire que la révélation fut close à la mort du
dernier des apôtres, si une croyance ultérieure ne s'y ratta-
chait pas par un lien vraiment rationnel et logique ?' (Boyer
[1940] p 265). The point is important, but it raises a question which cannot be satisfactorily answered so long as the
assumption persists that revelation consists simply in the
divine provision of propositions. De Lubac insists on the concrete unity of the experience of revelation: 'L'adhésion primitive au Christ fut une "perception toute concrète et toute
vivante", et nombre de dogmes restaient d'abord "latents
dans la richesse de cette perception première"' (de Lubac
[1948] p 155, quoting a phrase coined by Jules Lebreton in
1908). Revelation is the communication of the concrete
reality of God's self-gift in Jesus Christ. The content of revelation, he says, in a phrase reminiscent of Newman's insistence on the unity of the christian 'idea' (though not directly
derived from Newman), is 'le Tout du Dogme' (p 156).

This restatement of the problem, which was to influence
Rahner's studies in the years that followed, enables de Lubac
to stand the classic distinction between 'implicit' and 'explicit' revelation on its head, and by so doing to move very close
to Newman's position in the last of the *University Sermons*:
'contrairement à une affirmation courante qui est à la source
des difficultés que nous avons montrées, l'"implicite" n'est
contenu dans l'"explicite" comme tel. C'est, dès le début,
l'"explicite" qui est contenu dans l'"implicite", "dans la
frange définissable du mystère"' (p 158, quoting Simonin
[1935] p 552).

De Lubac's article marks a turning-point in twentieth-century studies of doctrinal development, although he explicitly refused to propose a 'theory' of development. For the remainder of this chapter, we shall consider one or two characteristic features of the work of three theologians who have made significant contributions to the problem in recent years: Karl Rahner, Edward Schillebeeckx and Bernard Lonergan.

The last point which we noted from de Lubac's article is similar to an important distinction which Rahner drew in an essay on doctrinal development first published in 1954: the distinction between 'formal statement' and 'formal communication'. Like de Lubac, he questions the widely held presupposition 'that the starting-point of a dogmatic explication is *always* a *proposition* in the proper sense' (Rahner [1961a] p 63). And he offers an illuminating analogy: 'Let us suppose that a young man has the genuine and vital experience of a great love, an experience which transforms his whole being. This love may have *presuppositions* (of a metaphysical, psychological and physiological kind) which are simply unknown to him. His love *itself* is his "experience"; he is conscious of it, lives through it with the entire fullness and depth of a real love. He "knows" much more about it than he can "state". The clumsy stammerings of his love-letters are paltry and miserable compared to his knowledge'. Yet even woefully inadequate verbal expressions may, in the concrete, 'communicate' to another person more than they succeed in formally 'stating'.

The church's concern, in 'developing' its doctrine, is not to acquire 'a sort of plus-quality of knowledge (as though the Church were somehow to become "cleverer")', but to find that expression of the reality of revelation which will be 'appropriate to just this age of the Church' (p 45). Much of Rahner's writing on the problem, until recently, remained within the 'cumulative', 'homogeneously evolutionary' framework which had dominated the discussion for over half a century. In this passage, however, we see an early indication of that shift of perception which will, when it is more thoroughly worked out by Rahner and others, bring catholic studies of doctrinal change and continuity into a discernibly closer relationship to protestant studies of 'hermeneutics'.

It is characteristic of Rahner that, while emphasising the inevitable inadequacy of any doctrinal statement, he rejects the idea that an inadequate expression of truth is 'half false'. 'Anyone who wants to call them "half false" because they do not state everything about the whole truth of the matter in question, would eventually abolish the distinction between truth and falsehood' (p 44). And, if changes in the cultural context demand changes in the expression of doctrine, it does not follow that 'the change is necessarily an abandonment of the earlier view or perspective . . . The mind of humanity, and even more of the Church, has a memory' (p 45).

Rahner tends to react rather sharply against the highly speculative and *a priori* nature of much that was written on doctrinal development during the previous period. But, in so doing, he is sometimes in danger of not leaving himself enough elbow-room for discerning and deploying criteria for critically evaluating contemporary or past developments. Thus, for example, he says that the 'possibility and limits of a development of dogma . . . must be arrived at inductively from the actual facts of such a development' (p 41). In order to avoid some of the difficulties to which such a position leads, he makes interesting and original use of the concept of the 'memory' of the church. If the church can be said to 'remember', it can also be said to 'forget'. 'The phrase, "forgotten truths", . . . must naturally be taken with a grain of salt. The Church's consciousness in faith always stores up more in her memory, as her lasting property, than is "present" to it at any particular moment in time which we may arbitrarily mark off. For the past and Tradition belong to this consciousness. But there will also be "forgotten truths" if it is true that the Scriptures and Tradition must be the ever new and inexhaustible source of theology' (Rahner [1963] p 135).

Another indication of the way in which Rahner was, at this time, opening up positions which would eventually destroy the assumption that the history of belief and doctrine could plausibly be conceived as a process of 'cumulative', 'homogeneous' development or 'expansion', is provided in a lecture which he gave in 1957. There he argued that, as well as being, from some points of view, a process of expansion, 'Dogmatic development must also contain a dynamism of compression and simplification, tending towards the blessed darkness of the one mystery of God' (Rahner [1966a] p 27). This line of thought is reflected in de Lubac's description, in a recent study, of the two tasks on which the church is permanently engaged by its use of the creed: 'Développement du dogme, approfondissement du mystère' (de Lubac [1969] p 242). We shall return to this suggestion in the following chapter.

In the same lecture, Rahner sets up an analogy between the move towards a dogmatic definition in the church, and the move towards the initial profession of faith on the part of an individual. The experience of faith, or conversion, entails and achieves a significant reorientation of perspective and understanding on the part of the individual. While the concept of a 'leap' of faith is notoriously problematic, it is undoubtedly the case that there is, in the concrete, a significant discontinuity between the conscious experience of one who has taken the decision of faith, and the one who has not. (This is by no means to suggest that either the decision, or its reflexive recognition, need be rapid or instantaneous processes). No decision 'is merely the execution of the judgement. It is also the coming of the light which alone can justify it in the measure in which it feels it must be justified in its own eyes. There is a mental clarity which does not precede the decision but can only be attained in the decision itself' (Rahner [1966a] p 31). We are here in the world of Newman's descriptions of the 'venture' or 'risk' of faith, and of Blondel's analysis of 'action' as a necessary condition for the discernment of truth.

When such a description is used as an analogy for the process whereby a dogmatic definition is arrived at, we should expect considerable emphasis to be placed on the fact that it is the *whole* church (and not just the defining authority) which is the subject of this process. Thus, according to Rahner, 'The Pope is the point at which the collective consciousness of the whole Church attains effective self-awareness, in a manner which is authoritative for the individual members of the Church . . . Hence the exercise of this authority—especially where it takes place in the service of dogmatic development—rests upon a clarification of the believing consciousness of the whole Church' (p 34). In the interests of discovering whether, in a given instance, an act of papal authority *is* such a 'clarification', we might also have expected some discussion of the role of the subsequent 'consent', or recognition of the authoritative act, on the part of the believing community as a whole. But this Rahner does not, in this lecture, provide.

From the middle of the nineteenth to the middle of the twentieth century, historical process was characteristically envisaged on the analogy of a 'stream', or the growth of an organism. In this context, the belief that the faith of each generation of christians was substantially identical with that of the generations which had preceded it, could be expected to take the form of a claim that the history of christian doctrine was a process of 'homogeneous evolution'. This, as we saw in the last chapter, is what in fact occurred. In recent years, however, the assumption of cultural homogeneity has withered away. Scholars in many disciplines have become increasingly conscious of the irreducible *pluralism* of human languages, thought-forms, and 'ways of seeing the world'. The 'world' in which each group, each individual lives, is the world as seen from a particular point of view. Increasing sensitivity to the fact of contemporary pluralism has made us newly aware that pluralism is no new phenomenon.

In other words, the viability of theories of the 'homogeneous evolution' of christian doctrine has been finally destroyed, not by 'denying' or 'disproving' them, but rather by the collapse of that assumption of cultural homogeneity which was their tacit presupposition. Rahner has seen this very clearly and, in an article written in 1969, has spelt out some of the implications for our understanding of dogma and of dogmatic development. In the recent past, some theologians envisaged, with enthusiasm, the possibility of a rapid succession of dogmatic definitions. But such a process 'presupposes that there is a common theology at everyone's disposal' (Rahner [1969c] p 56.) Therefore Rahner not only speaks of 'the cessation of such dogmatic developments', but says that 'we may well have to assume that in the future the magisterium will not be able to formulate new emphatic doctrinal pronouncements. Why? Because the unity of theology, which is the presupposition of such pronouncements, is no longer present'. The distinction between belief and the language of belief, between faith and theology, remains undoubtedly valid, but we are more conscious than earlier generations could have been that it is no easy matter to say today what was said yesterday, and to be certain that this is what we are saying. The 'grammar' of magisterial statements 'need not have been the one it is . . . it is influenced by historical, psychological and sociological factors' (p 54). Hence the impossibility of attempting to immunise the concepts employed in doctrinal statements from problems of hermeneutic and historical discontinuity: 'In former days, the statements of the Church's magisterium were the truly important theses of theology. This need not be the case for theology in the future. Indeed, it cannot be the case if theology is to perform its proper task . . . Attempts to present such theological concepts and their grammar as irreplaceable in the future—such as we seem to find in *Humani Generis* and *Mysterium Fidei*—are neither proper nor convincing.'

Apart from one or two studies, written in the early nineteenfifties, one of the strengths of Schillebeeckx's treatment of the problems with which we are concerned is that the standpoint from which he approaches them enabled him to avoid specific concentration on concepts such as 'development' and 'evolution'. Perhaps we can say that whereas Rahner had to effect, within his own theology, the shift from 'evolutionary' presupposition to a more episodic conception of cultural history, Schillebeeckx, several years younger, was more easily able to set his discussion of our problems within a broadly hermeneutical framework. Thus, an essay written in 1962 contained a section entitled: 'The question proper to dogmatics: the contemporary context of God's Word' (Schillebeeckx [1967] p 192).

Schillebeeckx 'prefers to call his subject the development of tradition rather than the development of dogma, so as to relate the dynamic handing on of revelation to the entire reality' (Schoof [1970] p 217). This is, of course, in harmony with the approach which we have recommended throughout this book. It also indicates that, in a statement such as the following, the term 'church' refers to the whole concrete reality of the believing community: 'The church does not derive its dogmas from theological conclusions drawn from Scripture, but it recognises its own living dogma in Scripture' (Schillebeeckx [1967] p 213).

Those theories of doctrinal development which stress the uniqueness of the process of tradition, and its substantial independence from the secular history of which it forms a part, not infrequently seem to assume that the concept of 'revelation' refers to some unusual, specifically religious type of experience. But, as Newman once said, 'When faith is said to be a religious principle, it is . . . the things believed, not the act of believing them, which is peculiar to religion' (P.S. 1 p 191). Similarly, Schillebeeckx introduces the concepts of 'revelation' and 'faith' as features of any situation in which human beings, in meeting each other, voluntarily emerge from their privacy to give themselves, to disclose themselves, to each other: 'in every case of truly human encounter between men, *revelation* and *faith* are present. It is only in an environment of love that this revelation and this faith acquire their full significance' (Schillebeeckx [1967] p 186).

We drew attention to Rahner's recent insistence on the fact that, since the concepts with which authoritative church pronouncements are expressed are socially and culturally conditioned, the task of theology, in a different cultural context, is to *replace* those concepts if the original affirmation is to be 'heard' in the new situation. This need to replace, or to relinquish, at least some aspects of the conceptual affirmation used to articulate christian belief in contexts different from our own led Schillebeeckx to speak 'of what he rather paradoxically calls "development through demolition". This idea did not emerge explicitly in Schillebeeckx's thought until just before the Council' (Schoof [1970] p 220).

Schoof, who has lucidly summarised the main features of

Rahner's and Schillebeeckx's thought on problems of
development (pp 212–221) remarks that, emerging from
different philosophical and theological schools, 'the ideas of
these two theologians converged in the period immediately
preceding the Second Vatican Council' (p212). It is significant that, whereas before the second world war, theologians
of their stature would probably have felt able to construct
full-fledged 'theories of development', neither of them has
done more than to offer 'perspectives for a synthesis' (Schillebeeckx [1967] p 81). Less *a priori* speculation, closer attention
to the complexities of doctrinal history, and an increasing
awareness of the sociological and psychological factors which
need to be taken into consideration, have combined to make
theologians more modest in their claims. In the last few years,
both Rahner and Schillebeeckx have given increasing attention to problems of doctrinal pluralism and (especially
Schillebeeckx) to problems of hermeneutic. In 1967, Schillebeeckx pointed out that the problems studied in catholic
theology under the rubric of 'doctrinal development' are,
fundamentally, the same problems which, in recent decades,
protestant theology has preferred to discuss in terms of
'hermeneutics': 'we can comprehend this biblical word in
faith only through a reinterpretative understanding of the
faith and in no other way. We cannot grasp the biblical text
directly "in itself", as though we, as readers or believers,
transcended time. This "thesis" is commonly held to have
originated with Bultmann and the theologians who followed
him, but in reality, though Catholics seldom seem to be
aware of the fact, it is one of the essential elements of Catholic theology. However, it has been presented theoretically not
in terms of "hermeneutics" but in terms of the "development
of dogma", which is the Catholic counterpart of what is
known in Protestant theology as the "hermeneutical" problem' (Schillebeeckx [1969] p 6).

Bernard Lonergan has written comparatively little that is
explicitly concerned with the problem of doctrinal development, although one would find much indirectly relevant
material in *Insight*, and in various essays on problems of
interpretation and cultural change. He did, however, tackle

the problem directly in the introduction to a Latin textbook on the theology of the Trinity.[1] More recently, he has returned to it in his important study of theological method (Lonergan [1972a].)

In the introduction to *Divinarum Personarum*, Lonergan discusses the classic notion of the *duplex via* by which man attempts to understand something of the mystery of God and, in the light of that mystery, to understand himself and his world. 'Starting from where we are', we explore, tentatively, into the mystery. This is the *via analytica*, or *via inventionis*. Then, on the return journey, as it were, starting (metaphorically) from the standpoint of the mystery, we try to see all things in their relationship to each other as totally dependent on that mystery. This is the *via synthetica*, or *via doctrinae*. These two 'movements' represent the 'God-ward' and 'man-ward' components of the task of theology. On the first way, reality appears as the 'image' of the God we seek to understand; on the second as the 'ex-pression' of the God in whom we believe. (Readers of *Method in Theology* will recognise that this distinction corresponds to that between the two 'phases' of theology—which is so central a feature of the book: 'If one is to harken to the word, one must also bear witness to it' (ibid p 133).

So far, medieval theologians would have felt quite at home. But we are conscious, as they could not have been, of the complexity and ambiguity of the idea of 'starting from where we are'. We are in very different places. The starting-point for exploration into God of a Jewish peasant, a Greek philosopher, a poor man in Cuba and a rich man in New York, will be very different, because their experience, their language, their 'world' will be so different in each case.

Therefore Lonergan includes a third 'movement' in theology, one which would have been unintelligible to the medieval mind: the 'historical movement' (cf Lonergan [1959] pp 28–41). He introduces the notion of 'trans-cultural shift' (*motus transculturalis*), to describe what takes place when ideas, knowledge, wisdom generated in one cultural context are transposed into another. Methodologically, it is important to notice that, in introducing this concept, Lonergan is not discussing an exclusively or even primarily 'religious' or theological problem, but the theological aspect of a completely general feature of the historicity of human ideas.

When a group of people attempt to transpose an idea, or set of ideas, from one cultural context to another, they find themselves obliged to consider new questions; questions that did not arise, and possibly could not have arisen, within the original situation. To the extent to which they succeed in answering these questions; to the extent, that is, to which they succeed in making the desired transpositions of meaning, they will have entered more deeply into truth. Therefore the process of trans-cultural shift brings with it a genuine increment in knowledge and wisdom. Lonergan is thus in a position to assert that, within the shift from one cultural 'starting-point' to another, in the history of belief and doctrine, there is also an element of 'development' in the sense of 'progress'. Even in his most recent study of the problem, this assertion has not been withdrawn. Lonergan still regards the asymptotic approximation to the 'goal of the complete explanation of all phenomena' (Lonergan [1972a] p 5), as the 'ideal' (p 128), not simply for method in the natural sciences, but also for theology. Even when acknowledging that 'The unity of a subject in process of development is dynamic' (p 138), he can still speak of 'the perfection of complete immobility', and he continues to conceive of 'Christian theology . . . as *die Wendung zur Idee*, the shift towards system, occurring within Christianity' (p 144).

Thus, although, on the one hand, by introducing the concept of the 'trans-cultural shift', Lonergan is in a position to take seriously the discontinuities in doctrinal history, he does not, on the other hand, abandon the conviction that there is an element of 'development', 'evolution', or 'progress' discernible in that history. If he has 'shied away from the word "evolution"', it is perhaps because of his awareness that a term which most easily evokes biological or organic imagery cannot do justice to 'historical process . . . [which] can only be adequately envisaged by means of an additional . . . strategy: dialectic' (O'Donovan [1969] p 142).

If, in *Method in Theology*, Lonergan's handling of our problems is not free from a certain ambiguity, this would seem to be partly due to the fact that he does not sufficiently re-

THE RECOVERY OF HISTORY

examine the concept of *revelation*. We have seen, again and again, that a theologian's handling of problems of doctrinal change and continuity is invariably dictated by the concept of revelation with which, or from which, he works.

There are several passages in the new book which indicate that Lonergan, like Schillebeeckx, now prefers to handle problems of doctrinal change and historicity within the framework of hermeneutics (though he prefers to restrict the *term* to the specific function of interpreting texts):[2] 'doctrines have meaning within contexts, the ongoing discovery of mind changes the contexts, and so, if the doctrines are to retain their meaning within the new contexts, they have to be recast' (Lonergan [1972a] p 305). He asks 'whether the doctrine of Vatican I on the permanence of the meaning of dogmas can be reconciled with the historicity that characterises human thought and action' (p 324). His answer is that 'What permanently is true, is the meaning of the dogma in the context in which it was defined. To ascertain that meaning there have to be deployed the resources of research, interpretation, history, dialectic' (pp 325–326). If he gives the impression of being remarkably sanguine about the possibility of ascertaining that earlier meaning with assurance; if, that is to say, he underestimates the herculean labour which is involved in successfully effecting the 'trans-cultural shift', this may be due to the intellectualism which continues to weaken his treatment of 'revelation' and 'dogma'. Revelation is still conceived almost exclusively as an 'original message . . . in which God has spoken to us' (p 295), and his assurance that we can overcome problems of doctrinal historicity is grounded in his conviction that 'dogmas . . . are not just data but expressions of truths . . . revealed by God' (p 325).

My concern in this chapter has simply been to give some idea of the way in which a few distinguished contemporary catholic theologians have approached problems of doctrinal change and continuity. We began this part with Newman. We have ended with Lonergan, whose thought owes much to Newman and, especially, to the *Grammar of Assent*. Within the last few years, the whole framework of the discussion has begun to shift. This has already become apparent during this chapter, because Rahner, Schillebeeckx and Lonergan have all contributed to this shift. In a final group of chapters, therefore, we shall try to indicate the present state of the questions with which we have been concerned.

NOTES

1. Lonergan [1959] pp 28–41. For an excellent study of Lonergan's thought, up to 1964, on doctrinal development, see Richard [1964].
2. 'The most striking feature of much contemporary discussion of hermeneutics is that it attempts to treat all these issues [ie problems of history, dialectics, foundations, doctrines, systematics and communication] as if they were hermeneutical. They are not' (Lonergan [1972a] p 155; cf pp 167–169).

PART FOUR

CHANGE IN FOCUS

15

PROGRESS OR CHANGING STRUCTURES?

'An historical crisis is a period in which the first principles that underlie a pattern of culture slowly die in the depths of collective consciousness. The relentless criticism of experience gradually reveals their inaptness to cope satisfactorily with the problems of life. The world built on them is at the end of its tether' (Walgrave [1972] p 31, summarising the thought of Ortega y Gasset). In any culture, men strive to order and structure the flow of experience. Experience is ordered, meaning is controlled, by the development of languages, value-systems and social institutions. According to Bernard Lonergan, who sees the present crisis as consisting in the collapse of 'classical', and its replacement by 'modern' culture, 'the classical thinks of the control as a universal fixed for all time; the modern thinks of the controls as themselves involved in an ongoing process' (Lonergan [1972a] p 29). In this situation, the erosion of absolutes that is experienced on all sides is seen by some as a liberation, by others as a threat to security and even to identity. Christian faith and christian theology have been heavily invested in the absolute, as a result not simply of their reference to an unchanging God, but also of the conviction of christian belief that the message of Jesus Christ is God's last, imperishable word to man. Therefore it is hardly surprising that problems of the relationship between faith and history should, during the past hundred years, have become increasingly central in theological debates.

'The problem of faith and history is not merely a problem of two logics or two methodologies. It is a problem . . . of two ethics of judgement . . . From liberal Protestantism to the new hermeneutic, Protestant theology may be regarded as a series of salvage operations, attempts to show how one can still believe in Jesus Christ and not violate an ideal of intellectual integrity' (Harvey [1967] p 104). For all the

grandeur and brilliance of these operations, it can hardly be
said that even the most distinguished of them was successful.
Thus, according to Harvey, 'Barth . . . claims all the advantages of history but will assume none of its risks' (p 158).
And it has been said of Bultmann that he 'fails to do justice
to the cosmic scope of . . . revelation, its relationship not
only to the existential life of the individual, but also to the
destiny of the whole world . . . All that is left of the whole
long process is a single point. . . . God's great drama has
become an "existentialist private performance"' (Zahrnt
[1969] pp 243-244, quoting Rudolf Bohren).

We saw in the last chapter that those theories of 'homogeneous evolution' which constituted the corresponding 'salvage operation', on the part of catholic theology after the
modernist crisis, have proved no more successful. We also
saw that, in the work of men such as Lonergan, Rahner and
Schillebeeckx, evolutionary and developmental models of
doctrinal history are gradually being replaced by a more
episodic view of history, which is more sensitive to the irreducible pluralism of that history, and which pays close attention to the problem of transposing meanings and values from
one cultural context to another. In these final chapters, therefore, we shall try to bring into sharper focus those aspects of
this shift in perspective which bear most directly upon the
problems with which we are concerned.

It is of the greatest importance continually to bear in mind
that this shift in historiographical perspective is common to
all areas of contemporary human inquiry. For a little over a
hundred years, western culture structured its experience of
history on evolutionary models. During this period, all
branches of historical study—in biology, or economics, or
physics, or politics, or theology—sought to discern, in the
past, the lines of development or evolution which had led to
the present. In recent decades, however, 'linear successions,
which for so long had been the object of research, have given
way to discoveries in depth'.[1] According to Foucault, recent
studies show that the history of an idea is not simply the
story of 'its progressive refinement, its continuously increasing
rationality, its abstraction gradient, but [rather] that of . . .
its successive rules of use, that of the many theoretical contexts

in which it developed and matured' (Foucault [1972] p 4). One of the reasons why it is difficult clearly to get into focus and to describe the shift that is taking place is that 'This epistemological mutation of history is not yet complete' (p 11).

Almost all theories of doctrinal development tend to assume that the history of christian doctrine is a more or less unified process of continual, if erratic, growth and expansion. We have seen how often the appeal has been made, on the basis of this assumption, to organic metaphors and analogies. Vincent of Lerins employed the image of plant growth in order to argue that nothing, fundamentally, had ever changed or ever could. In his biology, plants simply get larger. At the time of the reformation, catholic apologists used the image of growth from the initial 'seed' or 'germ', in order to justify the additions that had been made, in doctrine and practice, to what was explicitly contained in the 'plain words of scripture'. During the late nineteenth and early twentieth century, the image of organic growth was sometimes employed in such a way that christian origins, and in particular the new testament, were thought, in practice, to be of no more than genetic significance.

But there are two things that you can do to plants: you can allow them to grow, and spread all over the garden, or you can cut them back. Maurice Bévenot once suggested that the history of the church shows many instances where the process of development has been by way of pruning, rather than expansion. As illustrations of this, he suggests the doctrine of biblical inerrancy, the condemnation of usury, and the doctrine of the pope's primacy of jurisdiction. It may have been customary to consider doctrinal development 'as a kind of *expansion* of elements that were entrusted to the Church from the beginning, an expansion or fructifying of seeds of Christ's own planting . . . But "development" can take another form which has generally been overlooked. Instead of being an expansion, the fructifying of a scriptural plant, it can on the contrary be the *pruning* of some too vigorous growth' (Bévenot [1968] p 407). Speaking of the act of dogmatic definition, he says: 'Its instinct is sure enough, but it grasps its object only *grosso modo*, and can only express it in the categories and terms current at the time . . . in the course of time, much that seemed to be necessarily included in the definition, comes to be recognised as not belonging to that core of truth which was the real intention of the definition. In such a situation, through the *deeper understanding* of the mystery in question, the development takes the form of a pruning and purgation of the previous definition, so that what it has previously been obligatory to hold, as being included in that definition, can now be called in question or even denied' (p 408).

Bévenot's 'development by pruning' is not unlike Schillebeeckx's 'development by demolition', which we mentioned in the previous chapter. In that chapter, we also drew attention to Lonergan's claim that the process of translation demanded by the 'trans-cultural shift' led to deeper understanding because, in that process, new questions are necessarily asked and answered. But how are we to ensure that it is indeed the 'central core of truth' which is more deeply understood in the new context? What are the criteria on the basis of which certain aspects of the belief are now held to be disposable, as belonging simply to the original cultural context, as being 'husk' rather than 'germ'? There can be no general, *a priori* answers to these important questions. We shall return to them again. For the moment, it is sufficient to point out that the lines of thought suggested by Bévenot's article converge on that pursued by Bultmann in his original programme of 'demythologisation', a programme more appropriately described as one of 'deliteralisation' (Tillich [1967] p 228). Bultmann insisted that his intention was not reductionist: 'if we once start subtracting from the kerygma, where are we to draw the line? The mythical view of the world must be accepted or rejected in its entirety' (Bultmann [1964] p 9.)

But reductionism may take two forms. It sometimes consists of dismissing, as uncanonical, or irrelevant, or timebound, certain material elements in the field of data. Thus arguments could be produced for not bothering to transpose into the new context the message of the letter of James, or the narrative of the ascension. This is the reductionism which, in principle, Bultmann rejects. But there is another, and subtler form which is the result of restricting the range of questions which are put to the data. Thus if the only questions asked are questions which concern immediate existential significance then, even if those questions are put to the *whole* field of data, the answers will be correspondingly impoverished. In other words, the interpreter has to seek to put to the data whose meaning he would transpose into the new context, a range of questions broad enough to respect the richness and complexity of the manifold types of truth—factual, symbolic, descriptive, prescriptive, confessional—which the original set of statements expressed or embodied. We saw, in chapters 5 and 6, how often the history of christian doctrine has been the history of the impoverishment of an originally rich and complex reality because, in successive situations, only some questions and not others were put to the content of the tradition.

The claim that, as a result of 'pruning' or 'demolition', the 'core of truth' embodied in a statement of belief is 'more deeply understood' in the new context, is ambiguous: 'the real possession of revealed reality does not always necessarily grow, but can even diminish with the growth of the conceptual unfolding of what is attained in the actual act of faith' (Rahner [1966b] p 38). We are thus brought back to the point, of which Newman and Blondel were more sensitive than were many subsequent theologians, that the process usually referred to as the 'development of dogma', namely the accumulation of 'new' articles of faith, by no means necessarily entails a progressively deeper grasp, by the church, of that saving mystery to which its doctrine points. Only if it could be shown that the church has increased in holiness, in fidelity, could it said to have 'progressed', in any significant sense, in its grasp of saving truth.

If doctrines, rites or institutions which, in one cultural context, appropriately expressed or protected the central affirmations of christian belief, are simply carried over, 'untranslated', into a different context, then they become not merely useless, but harmful. In the new context they do not, and cannot, express the *same* meanings as they originally did. The merit of images such as Bévenot's 'pruning', or Schillebeeckx's 'demolition', is that they remind us that, if christian belief and christian living are to remain faithful to the gospel, then the process of tradition has to be seen as a process of continually attempting to appropriate, in successive cultural contexts, the 'fundamentals' of christian memory, hope, and loving obedience. We shall return to this consideration later in this chapter and, in chapter 16, it will lead us to make some final remarks about creeds and dogmas.

We suggested in chapter 10 that, in order to assess the 'truth' or faithfulness of a particular development in christian doctrine, it is necessary to ask whether the development in question expresses or embodies a style of life, an ethical response, which is in conformity with the style of life commanded or recommended by the gospel. But that 'style of life' is, in each successive situation (including the original one), as culturally embodied and particularised as are the statements and symbols of christian belief. Therefore, the task of 'translating' the tradition from one cultural context to another involves not simply *two* elements: the earlier and later doctrines, rites or institutions, but *four*: the earlier and later 'languages', and the earlier and later 'secular reality', or 'world', in which and for which the language is spoken. Within an apologetic framework, Newman recognised this when, in his long account of the 'first note' of a 'true development', he sought to compare the way in which 'the world now views [Christianity] in its age' with the way in which 'the world once viewed it in its youth' (Dev p 207).

The shift in historiographical perspective, to which I referred at the beginning of this chapter, has made us newly conscious that we can never acquire a 'bird's-eye view' of the historical process within which we are situated. Our own cultural context inexorably imposes limits on the questions that occur to us, the problems that strike us as urgent, and the techniques we employ in order to attempt to answer the questions and solve the problems. Because we are more aware than earlier generations of our 'situatedness', we are better able to appreciate that 'organic', evolutionary, linear descriptions of history were not so much 'objective' accounts of what had taken place, but were rather the way in which, in one particular cultural context, the inhabitants of that context ordered and interpreted their historical experience.

It does not follow that concepts such as 'development',

'evolution', and even 'progress', no longer have any place in the description of the process of tradition. My concern is less with specific historical description than with drawing attention to the dominant images, or paradigms, which characterise historical experience in different cultural contexts. To draw attention to the replacement of one dominant image by another is not to deny the unidirectionality of historical process, nor is it to rule out, *a priori*, the possibility that the historian may be able to discern elements of linear development or evolution in the history of this or that aspect of the tradition. But whereas against the background of evolutionary assumptions, particularities, discontinuities and radical change are not expected, and are frequently overlooked, a more episodic structuring of historical experience reverses this expectation. It is now the continuities, the 'developments', which become more difficult to discern and to establish. Moreover, in emphasising the need for total 'translation', or transposition, of the content of tradition from one cultural context to another, I am not recommending that 'transformism' which was repeatedly condemned at the time of the modernist crisis. In a situation in which evolutionary images (or even more static models surviving from a still earlier epoch) dominated, for a theologian to say that the content of tradition had undergone successive transformations was inevitably to invite the suspicion that he believed it to have undergone a *'metabasis eis allo genos'*. In a situation in which evolutionary assumptions no longer perform so pervasive and influential a role, a programme of 'total translation' may more easily be seen to be a *sine qua non* condition for the survival, in successive contexts, of the unchanging gospel.

It is not uncommon, today, for recognition of the inevitable discontinuity between our present experience and understanding, and that of an earlier generation, to generate a lack of interest in the past. As a result, many people try to solve the problems of today without reference to the problems of yesterday. But this is simply not possible. Our language, our symbols, our institutions, ourselves, are products of our past. To neglect that past, or to suppress it, leads not to liberation, but to a form of 'false consciousness' on the part of a society not unlike a neurotic condition on the part of an individual. The unending task of understanding the past, of recovering, or 'recollecting' those features of our past which we have forgotten or suppressed, is a necessary condition for understanding the present.

Nevertheless, as we have said already, although the past must be understood and appropriated, this can only be done from the standpoint of our present, concrete, culturally conditioned situation. As Jossua has pointed out, in an important study,[2] the idea of continual progress, in common with all systematic visions of history, seems incompatible with the way in which, in actual fact, we tackle historical problems, in that it seems to suppose an observer who stands at the end of history or who can fly along over its entire duration (cf Jossua [1968] p 180). Does it follow from this that we are condemned to a hopeless relativism in which all comparative assessments of christian belief and doctrine in successive cultural contexts are rendered impossible? Are we reduced to saying that the authors of the new testament said or believed A, the fathers B, the medievals C, ourselves D, and that this is all that can be said about it? One does indeed sometimes get the impression, from accounts of doctrinal history, that the author is so concerned to set statements in their historical context, so preoccupied with remembering that successive generations of christians were 'men of their time', that it seems almost impossible to introduce the notions of truth or falsehood into historical descriptions.

According to Jossua, our awareness of the historicity of christian truth, of the 'relationism'[3] to which we are inevitably subject, need not inhibit us from setting up some general models for understanding and evaluating doctrinal history. In order to describe the concrete unity of culture, language and faith at any given period, Jossua invokes the concept of 'structure'. Any such concrete structure is made up of two sets of components. On the one hand, there are all the various social, political, linguistic, religious and other factors which, in any historical or cultural context, influence the shape, the form, which is taken by belief, doctrine, or rite in this context. These he entitles the 'structuring elements'. On the other hand, there are the 'structured elements', the 'fundamental elements' of christianity, amongst which he includes: the *kerygma* (both the preaching of the message, and the message that is preached); certain 'key themes' or ideas which are seen continually to recur in successive situations; and the *questions* with which christians find themselves confronted, in their attempts to preach the gospel (*kerygma*), and to reflect on and appropriate the key themes, in each concrete situation.[4]

The model which Jossua offers is that of the interaction between the 'structuring elements', the changing situations in which the church exists, and the more or less constant factor of the 'structured elements': the message the church continues to preach, the themes and ideas with which it finds itself continually trying to grapple, and the questions to which its preaching and theology are the attempted, if inadequate and partial, response.

One obvious example of the 'key themes' of christian thought would be the consistent attempts to hold in tension the christian belief in the full humanity and full divinity of Jesus Christ; a theme which was given formal expression in the creeds of the great councils, and which has remained constant, as a central concern of christian theology, although the various ways in which it has been 'structured', in different times and places, have been very different one from another. Here one recognises the force of Lonergan's remark that the declaration of Nicea, while formally regulating the limits of christological discourse, 'leaves the believer free', so far as the material content of that discourse is concerned, 'to conceive the Father in scriptural, patristic, medieval, or modern terms' (Lonergan [1967b] p 345).

Another example would be what Jossua refers to as the 'anthropological paradox' (cf Jossua [1968] pp 186–188). Man is made for God, and is yet incapable of achieving that for which he is made, except as the acceptance of freely given salvation. This theme has been very differently 'structured' in the language and imagery of the new testament, in the distinctions of a later theology between 'nature' and 'grace', or 'creation' and 'redemption', and in contemporary attempts to reconcile man's full responsibility for the construction of his future with the affirmation that that future is in the mystery of God, the 'absolute future' of man.

There are a number of attractive features in Jossua's model of doctrinal history. In the first place, it avoids giving the impression that the history of christian doctrine is simply a process along which the believing community drifts, as it were, from one cultural context to another, with its beliefs, attitudes and institutions completely determined by the structuring elements of that culture (a danger not entirely avoided by a concept of 'historical necessity' such as that to which Loisy appealed). In the second place, it also avoids the opposite temptation of treating the history of doctrine as if it were more or less independent of, or at least not significantly affected by, the structuring elements. (This we have seen to be the temptation to which theories of 'homogeneous evolution' tended to succumb). In the third place, it draws attention to the fact that the christian attempt to preach the same gospel, and teach the same doctrine, is always a response to a challenge. In other words, christians experience, in each structured situation, the tensions that result from the interaction of gospel and culture. Thereby they are enabled to become conscious of the need prophetically to protest, within each situation, against those features of it which threaten to inhibit the hearing of the word, and the response to it in thought and practice. In the fourth place, discussing the problem of how the transpositions are to be made from one context to another, Jossua makes the important point that, although past structures may cease to be viable in the new context, they may retain a permanent value as 'models', reminding us of the elements that must not be lost sight of in the process of restructuring, and of the 'rules of structural balance' which relate those elements one to another (pp 184–185).

In order to indicate that approach to the problem of organising our christian historical experience which is displacing a dominantly evolutionary view of doctrinal history, we have so far made use of such concepts as 'development by demolition' (Schillebeeckx), 'trans-cultural shift' (Lonergan), 'development by pruning' (Bévenot), multiple *structurations* (Jossua). Gregory Baum prefers to speak of a 're-focusing of the Gospel. What do I mean by focus? Every age has its central questions; every age has its special way of being threatened and its own aspirations for a more human form of

existence . . . In every age, therefore, the Gospel is proclaimed with a central message and thrust, which is the saving
response of God to the self-questionings of men. This I call
the focus of the Gospel . . . as the old focus gives way to the
new, the entire doctrinal synthesis of the past falls apart in
order to be made anew in the light of the new focus' (Baum
[1968] pp 152–153). He insists that 'a focus of the Gospel is not
simply an important doctrinal position; it is, rather, the
central view, in the light of which the entire mystery of
salvation is understood and which holds together, interrelates,
and qualifies the entire teaching of the Church' (pp 170–
171).

One of the strengths of this description is that it indicates
that the changes in question are fundamental reorientations of
our christian experience and understanding. Provisionally, I
have from time to time referred to them as 'changes in perspective'. In fact, they go deeper than this visual analogy
suggests. They are changes in the manner in which we
experience and conceptualise the tradition we inherit.
This is not to say that, in the abstract, the 'laws of logic'
change from one age to another. But, in the concrete, the
differences between 'fields of argument' may be of greater
significance than formal logic is likely to appreciate (cf
Toulmin [1964]). Nor is it to deny that there may be formally
invariant structures of human cognition such that, in any
context, appeal may be made to Lonergan's 'transcendental
precepts. Be attentive, Be intelligent, Be reasonable, Be
responsible' (Lonergan [1972a] p 231). Nevertheless, if we
are sufficiently to appreciate the extent and pervasiveness of
the cognitional transformations that do, in fact, occur, we
need some phrase such as 'epistemic shift' (to adapt Foucault's
description).[5] Therefore, in chapter 17, we shall have to discuss the problem of the extent to which it is permissible, or
historically necessary, to speak of 'revolutions' in christian
doctrine and belief.

There is, however, an apparent weakness in Baum's position. He does not seem to take sufficiently seriously the
possibility that, however complete the 'refocusing' that takes
place, it may nevertheless be a refocusing of certain central
features, or fundamental elements, of christian belief. We have

seen that Jossua attaches considerable importance to the concept of 'fundamental elements'. He does not, however, directly tackle the question of the extent to which the articles of the creed, and solemnly defined dogmatic definitions may be said to be transculturally invariant, at least in the sense that no christian 'structure' would be complete which omitted any of them from its list of 'elements'. To the problem of creed and dogma, therefore, we must now return.

NOTES

1. Foucault [1972] p 3. 'Discoveries in depth', however, seems to miss the note of discontinuity, on which Foucault is insisting. The French text has 'un jeu de décrochages en profondeur'.
2. Jossua [1968]. A condensed and poorly translated summary of some of the themes in this article was published as Jossua [1970]. Our brief summary of some of the more important aspects of Jossua's article cannot hope to convey the subtlety, or the wealth of historical material, contained in the original.
3. According to Berger and Luckmann, Mannheim 'coined the term "relationism" (in contradistinction to "relativism")' to indicate that his approach to these problems in the sociology of knowledge denoted 'not a capitulation before the socio-historical relativities, but a sober recognition that knowledge must always be knowledge from a certain position' (Berger [1971] p 22).
4. 'La *structure* naît de la conjonction d'*éléments structurants* issus d'un contexte culturel donné, avec les *éléments fondamentaux* du christianisme: le *kerygma*, les idées-force que l'on va tenter de définir dans un instant, et les questions inévitables que d'âge en âge l'un et les autres font renaître' (Jossua [1968] p 177).
5. I have translated 'mutation epistémologique' as 'epistemic shift' because the change in question is only derivatively a change in epistemology, or the theory of knowledge. More basically, it is a change in the 'way we know', in our 'episteme'. When the term 'episteme' is used by Foucault himself, in his final chapter, it has a rather different connotation: cf Foucault [1972] p 191.

16

WHAT IS A DOGMATIC STATEMENT?

In writing the *Essay on Development*, Newman sought to construct a 'view' of doctrinal history according to which the church of Pius IX (and therefore its symbolic focus, or creed) could be seen to be the legitimate successor of the church of the fathers (and therefore of *its* creed). From within this perspective, any difference—of centrality or authority—between the 'articles' of the great creeds, and those other 'articles of faith' which were included, for example, in the Tridentine profession of faith, was obscured. Temporarily obscured, but not forgotten—as we can see from some remarks that Newman made seven years after the promulgation, by the Vatican Council, of the constitution *Pastor Aeternus*.

'The Apostles' Creed is rudimental: the so-called Creed of Pope Pius (IV) is controversial, and in this point of view is parallel to the Thirty-nine Articles, which no one would call a creed. We may call it Pope Pius's Creed improperly, as we call the Hymn *Quicunque* the Athanasian "Creed", because it contains what is necessary for salvation, but there can be but one rudimental and catechetical formula, and that is the Creed, Apostolic or Nicene' (V.M. 1 p 230).

From the point of view of the historical perspective which we adopted in the previous chapter, two fundamental questions emerge. Firstly: in order faithfully to 'translate' the creed ('Apostolic or Nicene') into our contemporary cultural context, will it be necessary to write a 'new' creed? Secondly: are there solemn papal or conciliar declarations of faith, beyond the apparent boundaries of the creed, of such lasting significance and authority for christian belief that they, too, must be transposed, as 'articles of faith', into our contemporary context, and not simply remembered as 'items on the agenda', as expressions of aspects of christian belief that must continually be borne in mind in our efforts to articulate, today, our christian confession of faith?

These two questions give rise to further questions concerning the unity, respectively, of creed, doctrine and scripture, and concerning the relationship of scripture to the confession of faith. So far as the latter problem is concerned, the recognition of the fact that the 'contradictionless doctrinal unity' which was formerly 'presupposed was not in fact present in the New Testament' (Pannenberg [1970c] p 193), suggests the possibility that we may need, not one 'new' creed, but several. In other words, is it impossible that the pluralism of the new testament should be reflected, in our more profoundly pluralistic world, by not one, but several 'forms of sound words'? If so, how are we to understand that unity of faith which the church continues to affirm and to seek?

Underlying all these questions there is the problem with which this chapter is immediately concerned: namely, what *sort* of statement is a 'dogmatic statement'? This problem must be tackled, unless we are willing to opt for a purely formal criterion, and say that any theological statement, regardless of its logical type, content or history, may be classified as a 'dogmatic statement', as binding on the faith of the individual christian, provided that it has been authoritatively proposed for belief by the appropriate authority. And to those lengths catholic theology, even in its most juridical moods, has never gone.

In recent decades, countless studies have been produced entitled 'What is a Dogmatic Statement?'. As with the concepts of 'revelation' and *magisterium*, the concept of 'dogma'— although frequently in need of apologetic defence against the nonbeliever—has only become an urgent theological problem, within 'the household of the faith', in our own day. As with so many of the topics which have concerned us, it was the modernists who asked the questions. Against the prevailing tendency, in catholic theology, to treat dogmatic statements almost exclusively as 'objective', descriptive propositions, the modernists insisted that they were personal, promissory responses to a revelation which is, fundamentally, a call to action. Against the prevailing tendency to appeal to such statements as if they were unproblematic descriptions, telling us directly 'what is the case' about God, the modernists stressed their inevitable inadequacy, insisted upon their symbolic nature, and underlined the apophatic dimension in all authentic human discourse concerning the mystery of God. To dismiss Tyrrell or Le Roy as 'pragmatists' or 'agnostics' would be to fail to take seriously the importance of those features of dogmatic discourse which they helped catholic theology to recover. Similarly, to dismiss the reigning scholasticism as crude, and fundamentally irreligious descriptivism, would be to underestimate that concern for rationality in religious discourse which it expressed, albeit in an impoverished manner.

We are in a position, today, to offer a more satisfactory answer to the question. 'What is a dogmatic statement'?, than either the modernists or their opponents were able to provide. In what follows, I shall make extensive use of an essay by the lutheran theologian, Edmund Schlink, which has exercised an extraordinary influence since it was first published in 1957, and which has won acceptance, at least in its broad outline, from both catholic and protestant theologians (Schlink [1967]). Our sketch of the history of the concepts of 'creed' and 'dogma', in chapter 6, should be kept in mind lest we forget that it is easier to discuss the elements of a dogmatic statement from the standpoint of systematic theology, than it is to decide which candidates for the title fulfil, or have fulfilled, the qualifications that would enable us to classify them as dogmatic statements. (It is useful to remember, for instance, how many propositions which, thirty years ago, were confidently listed, in manuals of catholic theology, as truths to be held *de fide catholica*, would now be classified far more circumspectly).

Schlink singles out four basic types of theological statement as 'the most elementary basic forms from the abundance of types of "responses of faith" contained in the Old and New Testaments': prayer, doxology, witness and doctrine. '*Prayer* is the response to the Gospel in which the divine "Thou" addresses us' (p 18). In prayer, the intersubjectivity of religious discourse is explicit; it is 'both the address of the divine "Thou" and the expression of the human "I"' (p 19). *Doxology*, or praise and adoration, 'is the reflection of the eternal divine majesty in human praise . . . It is, properly speaking, the theo-logical development of thankfulness for

God's action' (p 20). Here, the intersubjectivity is often only implicit. 'Neither the . . . worshipper nor his act of worshipping is explicitly mentioned in the words of the doxology . . . Hence doxological statements appear to be supremely objective' (p 22).

Whereas prayer and doxology are addressed directly to God, the other types of statement address our fellow-man. *'Witness* is the response to the Gospel which is directed to the "you" of our fellow-men' (p 22). As with prayer, the element of intersubjectivity is explicit in statements of witness. *Doctrine*, on the other hand, which is concerned both with the transmission of the tradition and with its interpretation, does not 'touch the individual human "you" in its actual historical situation with the same directness as does preaching' (p 26). Therefore, 'both doxological utterances and didactic formulas of teaching appear peculiarly "objective", though in different ways' (p 27).

According to Schlink, 'these basic statements of faith are the presupposition for all theological statements. Consequently a theological statement as such is not automatically a statement "about" God, but is primarily address to God, proclamation in God's name, confession and committal to him in worship' (p 32). The unique characteristic of credal or dogmatic statements consists in the fact that, in them, all four basic types of theological statement are combined: 'Owing to the peculiar concentration of all responses of faith in confession, one should not sharply distinguish between the confessional, hymnal, doxological, kerygmatic and didactic elements in any investigation of the origin of dogma' (p 34).

However, as we saw in chapter 6, this balance in credal structure was gradually lost sight of, especially in the west, and the doctrinal element began to dominate. Schlink illustrates this 'shift in credal structure from confession to doctrinal teaching' (p 35) by pointing out that the definition of Chalcedon begins, not 'We believe', but 'We teach'. And, as we remarked when commenting on this shift, the definition of Chalcedon never found its way into the liturgy. As a result of the tendency of doctrinal formulas to make equally 'objective' statements about 'everything which is expressed and realised in the acts of prayer, witness or doxology . . . these statements undergo a change of meaning in being objectified into didactic form' (p 40).

Schlink insists that the 'statements of doxology are ultimate' (p 42). This is why Pannenberg, following him at this point, says that credal statements 'cannot be directly employed as premisses for drawing out logical consequences' (Pannenberg [1970c] p 203). The key word is 'directly'. Neither Schlink nor Pannenberg denies that the christian confession of faith demands, as one of its presuppositions, the possibility of making certain historical judgements; neither of them denies that the possibility of making 'objective' statements, concerning what is in fact the case, is necessarily implied by confessional discourse. To insist on the primacy of the doxological element in credal and dogmatic discourse is not to reduce the use of the creed to a 'declaration of attitude' (Le Roy [1918] p 63). Rahner's warning that 'le concept de doxologie (tel que, par exemple, le défend E. Schlink) ne peut être l'*unique* facteur structurel sur lequel reposerait la confession de foi au Christ' (Rahner [1969b] p 242, my stress) was necessary only because there had been a tendency disastrously to oversimplify Schlink's analysis.

Dogmatic statements, then, combine, in their structure, the elements of doxology, prayer, witness and teaching. As such, they form the nucleus of the verbal articulation of christian faith, and their normal context is the liturgy in which that faith is celebrated; in which christian memory and hope achieve their paradigmatic expression. The creed, 'Apostolic or Nicene' is, in most streams of christian tradition, the central and normative unit of dogmatic statements.

In the life of the church, the creed needs continually to be interpreted. This day-to-day teaching of the church has a twofold purpose: it enables christians of every age and culture to appropriate their faith, and it protects that faith against error. In our own day, the positive task of interpretation is especially difficult, because of the bewildering variety of cultural contexts, and philosophical climates, in which christians live. So far as the protective function of teaching is concerned, perhaps we could suggest that, today, it is likely to be exercised especially in three directions: in insisting that there is an irreducible element of historical facticity in the ground of

christian belief; in affirming that, however anthropocentric or
'subject-centred' the starting-point of christian theology, it
does point beyond man to the absolute mystery of God; and
in reminding christians, again and again, that their confession
of faith has practical, social and political implications.

At this point we must return to the two questions which I
asked at the beginning of this chapter. Firstly: in order faithfully to translate the creed into our contemporary cultural
context, is it necessary to create 'new' creeds, or short formulas
of faith? There can be no argument, in principle, against the
propriety of replacing one formula by another. Moreover, it
could be argued that, in their existing form, the ancient creeds
require so thorough a programme of continual interpretation
as to make their retention counterproductive. On the other
hand, their antiquity enables them to speak powerfully of
christian continuity, and their symbolic richness renders
them patient of a wide variety of legitimate interpretations,
whereas almost every 'new' formula that has been attempted
is more immediately the expression of a particular theological
school or philosophical position. Thus, for example, Alex
Stock has pointed out that 'Our reflections on Rahner's short
formulas have shown that they are only intelligible if one is
already familiar with Rahner's theological system as a whole.
They are an extremely compressed summary of the approach
and logic of his theology' (Quoted Beirnert [1972] p 75).

The way to a solution, I believe, is to be found in the realisation that the church does not need to focus its belief in one
single formula. 'At least until the conversion of Constantine
. . . the recitation of identical credal formulas was not considered essential to Christian fellowship' (Dulles [1968] p 408).
And the argument of Schlink's study leads up to 'the basic
assertion that the unity of dogmatic statements need not consist in the acceptance of one and the same formula, since it can
also exist in the mutual recognition of different dogmatic
formulas' (Schlink [1967] p 80). So far as the eucharistic
celebration of faith is concerned, I have argued elsewhere that
there are grounds for suggesting that christians who use what
they mutually recognise to be the same creed are not sufficiently divided in belief as to justify the maintenance of 'separate
tables' (cf Lash [1973]).

In other words, the answer to our first question would seem to be that new credal forms are certainly desirable, and probably necessary, but that there are sound reasons for suggesting that, once we return to the ancient practice of employing a variety of mutually accepted formulas, the Apostolic and Nicene creeds should be included in their number: 'No formulary has a claim to exclusive use in the Church' (Beirnert [1972] p 76).

Our second question was more immediately concerned with the problem of 'dogmatic development' in the strict sense. We asked whether there are solemn papal or conciliar declarations of faith, of such lasting significance and authority for christian belief that they, too, must be transposed, *as* 'articles of faith', into our contemporary context. Another way of putting the question would be to ask whether some, or all, of these 'dogmatic definitions' (one thinks of some of the canons of Trent and Vatican I, and of the two modern 'marian dogmas') answer to the description that we have offered of a dogmatic statement.

Adequately to answer this question it would be necessary to examine, in detail, each of the doctrines in question, in the historical, theological and social context of their original declaration. All that is possible here is to suggest a few general principles which should be taken into account in any such examination.

1. In the first place, any argument to the effect that the application of purely formal, juridical criteria elaborated late in the history of catholic christianity can, of itself, solve the problem would be theologically inadequate and historically unconvincing. Our brief glance at the history of the concepts of *fides* and *magisterium* should be sufficient to show how anachronistic such a procedure would be. Not that formal criteria are unimportant: they remind us that it is to the holders of apostolic office, and not to the theologians, that the responsibility of authoritatively declaring the faith of the church ultimately belongs.

2. In the second place, I would wish to argue that inclusion in the creed is a necessary condition without the fulfilment of which the statement of a particular aspect of christian doctrine cannot be said to be a 'dogmatic statement' in the full

sense. Now it is certainly not unthinkable that new credal formulas should contain certain propositions not found in older creeds. After all, even the Apostles' Creed was not originally intended 'to be regarded as the quintessential summary of the whole of christian dogma. It only includes those main truths, a confession of which was required of catechumens' (Schillebeeckx [1967] p 231). The Apostles' Creed only came to be regarded as a 'quintessential summary' at a period when the essential unity of the creed had been lost sight of. The 'twelve articles' of the creed were thus put to a pedagogic use not unlike that which the 'ten commandments' served, for a long period, in relation to the church's ethical teaching.

'One thing alone', said Newman, 'has to be impressed on us by Scripture, the Catholic idea, and in it [all the propositions of Catholic doctrine] are included' (U.S. p 336). To appeal to the unity of scripture, or to the unity of the creed, is to remember that christian belief is not a matter of assenting to a number of separate 'truths'. It is the attempt intelligibly to articulate the experience of christian faith, an experience in which both memory and hope are continually referred to the one mystery of Christ as their origin and fulfilment. The *fides quaerens intellectum* thus continually seeks to unify all our experience and understanding, 'secular' as well as 'religious', in the light of that one mystery. Before a new article is included in the creed, therefore, the church must agree that its inclusion is in some way necessary for the church's confession, today, of the mystery of Christ.

Earlier in this chapter, we argued that the pluralism of the cultural contexts in which christians today seek to live their faith demands the use of several credal formulas, in the 'mutual recognition' of which the church's unity in belief was maintained and fostered. In view of the fact that these formulas will express very different philosophical, methodological, theological and spiritual attitudes and concerns, it seems not impossible that one church should continue to be able to recognise the face of Christ in the creed of another church, considered *as a whole*, even if the latter should include some particular statements which could not easily be included as dogmatic statements in the former.

3. If we bear in mind the fundamentally doxological character of dogmatic statements, it is clear that any such statement must be capable of being used as an act of worship, of God's glory, and not merely as a statement 'about' God or his dealing with men. Therefore, any doctrine which cannot be so used, but which *only* exercises a protective or interpretative (didactic) function, cannot be classified as a dogmatic statement in the full sense.

According to this criterion, it would seem, at least at first sight, that the two modern marian dogmas, of the immaculate conception and the assumption, could be so classified. It can be argued that, in their deepest intention, they affirm the eschatological nature of Christ's death. They affirm of Mary that which the church has always affirmed of mankind *as a whole* in the light of Christ's resurrection, but which cannot be affirmed of any other *particular individual* as clearly and straightforwardly as it can of her (cf Rahner [1961b, c, 1967]). They confess 'the forgiveness of sin, the resurrection of the body, and life everlasting': 'In the most holy Virgin the Church has already reached that perfection whereby she exists without spot or wrinkle' (*Constitution on the Church*, 65). They are undoubtedly 'symbolic' statements, since they could not be used of Mary were she not seen as the 'type' of the church. But this does not mean they are not true. It would seem, therefore, that they are candidates for possible, but not necessary, transposition, *as* articles of faith, into a changed cultural context.

Paradoxically, the application of the same criterion seems to lead to the conclusion that specific doctrinal assertions concerning the eucharist (such as certain canons of Trent, for example) do not need to be regarded as candidates for inclusion in the creed, and classification as dogmatic statements. This is not because the church's beliefs concerning the eucharist are peripheral or unimportant. Quite the contrary. The eucharist is the central, privileged context in which christian faith is affirmed and celebrated. In that celebration, by that celebration, the *whole* faith of the church is confessed in a complex dramatic unity that is at once prayer, doxology, witness and teaching. Specifically eucharistic doctrine is protective or interpretative of the meanings embodied and confessed in the celebration itself.

4. A possible fourth criterion concerns the historical reference of any doctrine whose candidacy for the status of 'dogmatic statement' is under discussion. But how is this 'historical
reference' to be understood in particular cases? In mariology,
according to Pannenberg, 'the church has not, as in Christology, pursued the inner logic of a historically given starting
point, but has sought repeatedly to express its own essence
in the figure of Mary. This distinction should certainly
suggest the fact that there can be no Marian dogmas in the
sense that there are Christological dogmas upon whose
acceptance or rejection the salvation of the individual depends.
For the same reason, no dogmatic necessity can be ascribed
to Mariological statements. To place them parallel to and on
an equal level with Christological statements' would preju-
dice 'the uniqueness of the history of Jesus Christ' (Pannenberg [1968] p 147).

That marian doctrine and piety have frequently taken
forms which appeared to threaten the uniqueness of that
history need not be denied. But is that all that needs to be
said? The root issue here, once again, is the unity of the
creed and of the set of dogmatic statements. All theological
statements derive their specifically christian intelligibility
from their reference to, and dependence on, the mystery of
Christ. Thus any dogmatic statement is only able to be such
in so far as it is, in some sense, a christological statement.
As we said in chapter 6, the christian affirmation arises out of
the experience of life in the Spirit of Christ, in which the
Lordship of Christ—which points beyond to the mystery of
the Father—is confessed. The term 'christological statement'
should be taken to refer, not simply to the 'second article' of the
creed, but also to the first and third (and it is in the third
article that, we have suggested, the doctrines of the immaculate conception and the assumption should be located).

In view of these considerations, our fourth criterion needs
to be restated. It is undoubtedly the case that any dogmatic
statement, as a statement not only of hope but also of memory,
must have an historical reference. But this historical reference
is sometimes (as in the case of the creatorship of God) not
given directly, but only indirectly, through the relationship
of the doctrine to that christological context in which alone

every aspect of christian doctrine finds its specifically christian intelligibility. (If it is reasonable to suggest that the historical reference of the doctrines of the immaculate conception and the assumption is, in this sense, indirect, there are other cases —such as that of the doctrine of the virginal conception of Jesus—the exact nature of whose historical reference is currently subject to enquiry and possible reassessment: cf Brown [1972].)

I insisted, at the outset, that I was only concerned, in this chapter, with proposing some general principles in the light of which our second question should be tackled. I have suggested that the subject of a solemn ecclesial decision, by pope or council, is only to be regarded as a 'dogmatic statement' in the full sense, in so far as it may be included in the church's creed, may be cast in the form of an act of praise or worship, and is located in the context of the church's understanding of the one mystery of Christ.

In modern times, due to excessive reliance on formal, juridical criteria, catholic theology has tended to work with a univocal concept of 'dogma' which is theologically inadequate, historically unconvincing, and ecumenically unfortunate. If the class of dogmatic statements, in the strict sense, is far more restricted than catholic theology has, in modern times, frequently supposed, it does not follow that all other elements of church teaching may simply be regarded as having been relegated to the status of 'opinions', to be accepted or rejected at the whim of the individual. It may well be the case that, in particular historical circumstances, the church is able, and indeed obliged, to exercise its interpretative and protective doctrinal function with such clarity and conviction that, although the doctrine that is thus declared cannot be regarded as a dogmatic statement in the full sense, it may nevertheless be recognised in the church as indubitably true. If so, then it must remain 'on the agenda', even when the cultural and theological context change dramatically,

Such an authoritative doctrinal declaration need not continue to occupy, in the new situation, that prominent place which it rightly occupied in the situation which called it forth. But it must be 'remembered', and therefore the effort must be made to 'translate' it into successive cultural contexts, in order to discover whether, when thus translated, it still 'says something' of immediate doctrinal and pastoral significance.

'In its desire for statements of eternal validity, Dogmatics has often lightly passed over the problem of identity and validity in the variety of historical statements which were made in changing historical situations' (Schlink [1967] pp 72–73). In these chapters, we have been trying to outline an approach to these problems which does not 'pass them over lightly'. It is undoubtedly the case that, as we suggested in chapters 8 and 10, catholic discussion of the concept of 'infallibility' has been inextricably bound up with that historical, philosophical and theological perspective, or *epistemé* which, it has been my contention, is being replaced by a radically different patterning of our historical experience and conceptual understanding. The task of transposing the 'core of truth' (to use Bévenot's phrase) in the doctrine of 'infallibility', into our new cultural context, is immensely complex, and certainly incomplete. In conclusion, I would only wish to suggest that nothing in the approach which I have so abstractly sketched in this chapter seems to be in fundamental disagreement with the position adopted by Congar in his nuanced critique of Hans Küng's study of infallibility (cf Congar [1970c]).

Not the least important feature of Congar's treatment is his insistence that the notion of truth to which one is appealing when making the claim that dogmatic statements are perennially true is not simply that notion correlative to their didactic or descriptive function, but also, and more fundamentally, the truthfulness, the fidelity of God (cf Lash [1971a] p 108). In the present context, I wish to suggest that the same consideration applies to those interpretative or protective declarations which, even though they do not qualify as dogmatic statements in the full sense, yet brought into play, at the time of their pronouncement, the full weight of the teaching authority in the church and were so recognised or 'received', subsequently, by the believing community as a whole. If this is so, then the christian community is entitled to trust that such doctrines will never be shown to have been simply false. Therefore, they remain 'on the church's agenda', even though their *use* might, in some other context, lead—in practice— to a distortion of christian thought and action. 'Ma position est nette: "infaillible" ne s'applique qu'à certains *actes*, dans des conditions bien délimitées . . . Il s'agit de jugements sur des points mettant en cause la vérité du rapport religieux. Dieu s'est engagé en vertu de *Sa* fidélité à l'Alliance' (Congar [1970c] p 616).

17

REVOLUTION AND CONTINUITY

In an essay first published in 1948, Bernard Lonergan claimed that 'the development of Christian doctrine is not subject to the revolutions that are part and parcel of the development of science' (Lonergan [1967a] p 76). And Walgrave, although he admits that 'the development of Christian doctrine in history . . . is subject to all the conditions that a good sociology of thought discovers in the general history of ideas' (Walgrave [1972] p 382), claims that it is 'insane . . . to conceive the great historical stages of human development as closed compartments, so that a man can no longer think the things that were thought by past generations' (p 276). Those two claims indicate the two aspects of the problem which we wish to discuss in this final chapter. In the first place, we suggested in chapter 15 that the discontinuities between successive cultural contexts, the 'epistemic shifts' that occur in the course of the process of tradition, are sometimes sufficiently profound as to raise the question: are there not features of doctrinal history which it would be misleading, or merely pedantic, *not* to describe as 'doctrinal revolutions'? In the second place, if we decide that we must speak , not only of 'evolution', but also of 'revolution', in christian doctrine, and if the history of revelation is subject to all the conditions that prevail in the general history of ideas, is it not then a mistake too readily to assume that we *can* 'think the things that were thought by past generations'?

Since, in 1948, Lonergan admitted the occurrence of revolutions in scientific history, while denying that they take place in the history of doctrine, he has become increasingly interested in similarities between theological and scientific method. He does not (as some of his critics have maintained) conceive of theological method on the analogy of scientific method (cf his rebuttal of Gilkey in Lonergan [1971] pp 224–225), but he does claim that, methodologically, theology and natural science have certain common features, in virtue of their common grounding in what he calls 'transcendental method'. His invocation of 'transcendental method' is similar to Walgrave's appeal to 'the basic structures of the human mind' (Walgrave [1972] p 276). Some such appeal is undoubtedly important, if we are not to resign ourselves to the impossibility of all historical understanding (cf Pannenberg [1970a]), but it can only be 'cashed', in the concrete, tentatively and often with considerable difficulty.

According to Lonergan, 'method', whether in science or theology, 'is a normative pattern of recurrent and related operations yielding cumulative and progressive results' (Lonergan [1972a] p 4; cf pp 14, 20, 43, 201). We have already seen that the assumption that theology yields 'cumulative and progressive results', an assumption which contributed to the creation of theories of 'homogeneous evolution', is yielding to the view that doctrinal history is better described as 'a series of formulations of the one content of faith diversifying and finding expression in different cultural contexts' (Congar [1970a] p 87). Similarly, in the natural and social sciences, the assumption that scientific method yields 'cumulative and progressive results' has been increasingly challenged. It has been shown to be in need of rather drastic qualification. In turning to Thomas Kuhn's *The Structure of Scientific Revolutions* as an initial illustration of this shift, it is only fair to warn the reader that Kuhn's thesis has by no means met with universal acceptance amongst historians and philosophers of science, and that it is not without its imprecisions and ambiguities— not all of which have been removed by the debate that followed its publication. Nevertheless, both the book and the debate are important indications of a shift in scientific historiography and epistemology that has striking similarities with that which has concerned us in the last few chapters.

Scientific textbooks have long given the impression that the development of science has been linear and cumulative. They give no hint of the possible occurrence of revolutions in scientific method. Yet 'in recent years . . . a few historians of science have been finding it more and more difficult to fulfil the functions that the concept of development-by-accumulation assigns to them' (Kuhn [1962] p 2). This group of historians have become convinced, as historians, that another model is needed to illuminate otherwise inexplicable features of the history of science (In the following paragraphs, I have made use of material first published in Lash [1971c]).

Kuhn introduces two key technical concepts. The first is that of the scientific 'paradigm': paradigms are 'universally recognized scientific achievements that for a time provide model problems and solutions to a community of practitioners' (p x). The second is that of 'normal science', which he describes as the state of scientific theory and practice during the period in which a given paradigm is in unquestioned possession. Positively, the effect of the paradigm is to enable scientific inquiry to proceed with assurance and success; negatively, the assumptions of the paradigmatic perspective, and the 'rules of the game' which they dictate, inevitably restrict the range of questions that are asked, and techniques that are employed. But a time comes when more and more problems crop up which resist solution by the techniques available under the influence of the paradigm. The 'rules of the game' begin to be questioned and challenged, and scientific discovery moves towards a state of crisis. 'All crises begin with the blurring of the paradigm and the consequent loosening of the rules for normal research' (p 84). If all goes well the outcome of the crisis is the replacement of one paradigm by another. This process, which Kuhn describes as a 'paradigm-shift', is not a matter of seeing some new thing, but rather of seeing all things newly. As a simple parable, he invokes Wittgenstein's 'duck-rabbit': 'What were ducks in the scientist's world before the revolution are rabbits afterwards' (p 110). Once the paradigm-shift has taken place in the scientific community as a whole, a new state of 'normal science', with a different set of presuppositions, techniques and methods, is arrived at.

So much, in outline, for the thesis. Now for a number of corollaries. In the first place, there is the tendency, once the paradigm-shift is fully achieved, and forgotten, to look back over the history of science and to imagine that 'it has ever been thus'. But, as Kuhn reminds us, 'Scientists are not . . . the only group that tends to see its discipline's past developing linearly towards its present vantage. The temptation to write history backwards is both omnipresent and perennial' (p 137).

In the second place, 'The transfer of allegiance from paradigm to paradigm is a conversion experience that cannot be forced' (p 150). In the third place, 'We . . . have to relinquish the notion . . . that changes in paradigm carry scientists and those who learn from them closer and closer to the truth' (p 169). In other words, it is not only in theology, but also in the history of natural science, that 'a more refined solution to the problem of progress . . . must be sought' (p 169).

Kuhn's critics have tried to discredit the concept of a 'scientific revolution' on the grounds that, if you look closely enough, the changes in question are patient of a gradualist interpretation. But, 'we do not treat tidal waves as special cases of erosion . . . revolutions are no more total in science than in other aspects of life, but recognising continuity through revolutions has not led historians or anyone else to abandon the notion' (Kuhn [1970] p 250).

If we acknowledge the occurrence of scientific revolutions, what basis of comparison is available from which to assess theories elaborated before and after such a revolution? Kuhn denies that there is available a 'neutral observation language', on the basis of which competing theoretical interpretations could be compared. 'If I am right', he says, 'then "truth" may, like "proof", be a term with only intra-theoretic applications' (p 266). If we reject, with Kuhn, the notion of a 'neutral observation language', then, I suggest, we shall be obliged to agree with him that 'Successive theories are . . . incommensurable' (p 267). To say that two theories are incommensurable is not to say that all hope of translation is doomed to failure from the start. But it is at least to say that 'People deeply committed both to accuracy and to felicity of expression find translation painful, and some cannot do it at all. Translation . . . always involves compromises which alter communication' (pp 267–268). Others would go further. Paul Feyerabend, for instance, 'wholeheartedly accept[s]' what he takes to be Kuhn's assertion that 'succeeding paradigms can be evaluated only with difficulty and that they may be altogether incomparable, at least as far as the more familiar standards of comparison are concerned' (Feyerabend [1970] p 219).

The similarities in the shifts that are taking place in theological and scientific conceptions of history are neither coincidental, nor are they to be accounted for on the hypothesis that theologians and scientists have been closely collaborating. It would be nearer the truth to say that there has been, in both theology and the history of science, a shift in what is regarded as the appropriate concept of rationality—and hence of 'proof' and 'evidence'. Thus Kuhn describes his and Feyerabend's work as 'an attempt to show that existing theories of rationality are not quite right and that we must readjust or change them to explain why science works as it does' (Kuhn [1970] p 264). This suggestion deserves exploring in rather more detail.

Collingwood's *Idea of History* is a polemical book because its author was fighting for the automony of historical method. It had come to be assumed that the paradigm of good method was what the physicist did. And the physicist—at that period —tended to assume that what he did was to interpret 'the facts'—out there, in front of him—with olympian detachment and 'objectivity'; science prided itself in being 'value-free'. The paradigm for 'rational' proof, argument and explanation was what the physicist thought that he was doing. (At that time, the paradigm of sound theological method was often similarly conceived, in neo-scholastic circles, as the deduction of universally valid 'truths' from the 'facts' of biblical texts or conciliar pronouncements).

Collingwood fought for the autonomy of historical method. But there are other disciplines, sociology and anthropology for example, that still tend to live under the shadow of the assumption that physics is the paradigmatic science. Thus Winch has felt obliged to attack that 'conception of the relation between the social studies, philosophy and the natural sciences', according to which the social scientist 'must follow the methods of natural science rather than those of philosophy if [he is] to make any significant progress' (Winch [1970] p 1). It is interesting to notice that the title 'exact science' is still restricted to those disciplines whose procedures are quantifiable. But mathematical expression is not the only form of conceptual clarity and precision—as every poet knows. For many natural scientists, sociology and anthropology are poor relations—muddy in their method, and only by some generous analogy to be spoken of as science. Thus Karl Popper, referring to sociology and psychology, speaks of 'the regress to these often spurious sciences' (Popper [1970] p 58).

In other words, the shift that is taking place in scientific historiography may be ascribed to the recognition that the history of a scientific theory cannot restrict itself to an account of successive formulations of the theory in the writings of a few outstanding scientists. Some historians of science have come to appreciate the importance of extending the field of relevant data (and therefore paying attention to the work of the sociologist.) They have come to see that the history of ideas must be the concrete history of the body of people who held the ideas, and of the social contexts in which they lived and worked. It has, I hope, been sufficiently demonstrated by now, in the course of this book, that a similar 'conversion to the concrete', a similar broadening of the field of relevant data, has been a distinctive characteristic of recent developments in theology. Perhaps we could put the matter very briefly by saying that theologians and historians of science have shifted their centre of interest from concentration on the argument to concentration on the men who argue.

We saw that one of the consequences of admitting the concept of 'revolution' into our description of the history of ideas is that it discloses the problem of incommensurability. How do we compare statements, attitudes, patterns of language, imagery and argument, generated in significantly different cultural contexts? Underlying this question there is a more basic one. Once we admit that certain of our christian predecessors may, because of the cultural discontinuities which separate them from us, be *strangers* to us, we have to ask the question: how do we understand a stranger? It may be 'insane' to maintain that 'a man can no longer think the things that were thought by past generations', but it is surely evident that we find it no easy matter to share the conscious experience, attitudes, hopes and understanding, of a first-century Jew, a fourth-century Greek, a medieval Frenchman, or even an eighteenth-century Englishman?

For sociology and anthropology, today, a central methodological question is, precisely: can we understand a stranger? There is at least one obvious difference between the form in which the problem emerges for the anthropologist, and the

form in which it emerges for the historian—whether of doctrine or of science. For the anthropologist, the relationship
between the inquirer and the stranger is synchronic: he can
take his tape-recorder and ciné-camera out to Brazil, and
obtain reactions from the stranger whom he hopes to understand. For the historian the relationship is diachronic; and
the dead cannot answer back. Nevertheless, we too, as theologians, have a synchronic dimension to our problem of the
apparent incommensurability between different cultural contexts. In the previous chapter, we recommended the use of
several different credal formulas of belief to enable one faith
to find pluralistic expression. But we have to face the problem:
how are we to find a route between the Scylla of an abstract,
artificial uniformity of expression, and the Charybdis of a relativism which would decline all responsibility for approving
some forms of belief, and disapproving of others? To what
extent can we, and should we tolerate the admission that our
brother in Christ is a stranger whom we cannot understand?
I have suggested that, strategically, an answer to such questions may be indicated by the concept of 'mutual recognition'.
This does not solve any of the problems, but it does suggest
the direction in which a solution may be sought.

How do we understand a stranger? We have insisted,
throughout this book, on the importance of situating theological statements in the concrete context in which they were
first produced. To conclude the present section, I propose
briefly to indicate that the implementation of this rubric is not
quite so unproblematic as some people seem to imagine.

Let us suppose that a theologian is studying Boniface VIII's
bull *Unam Sanctam*. There he reads: 'Porro subesse Romano
Pontifici omni humanae creaturae declaramus, dicimus,
definimus et pronuntiamus omnino de necessitate salutis'
(Denzinger 469). He translates this as: 'We declare, announce,
define and proclaim that subjection to the Roman Pontiff is
absolutely necessary for salvation, for every human being'.
There, surely, is an *ex cathedra* papal definition if ever there
was one, and it seems to be manifestly false. Then the theologian remembers the importance of understanding any statement in its historical context. He discovers that the problem
to which the pope is addressing himself is not any theoretical

theorem in soteriology or even ecclesiology, but a conflict concerning the respective socio-political authority of the pope and the king of France. Boniface VIII wishes to assert the transcendence of God's kingdom—in relation to which all human community is provisional and subordinate. The theologian therefore recasts the papal definition in terms which take these considerations into account and, accordingly, is able to assess it as meaningful and true.

This sounds fine but, in fact, it is not what usually happens. Very often, 'it is the *prior* determination that [the stranger's statement] be interpreted favourably, which determines just how much context will be taken into consideration' (Gellner [1970] p 33). In other words, in setting out to translate the stranger's statement, 'the prior disposition concerning what kind of interpretation one wishes to find, determines the range of context brought in'. In the case of *Unam Sanctam*, the dominant concern that drove the theologian to seek the contextually broader translation may not have been the disinterested purity of sound hermeneutical method, but rather the antecedent conviction that popes do not define error. The lesson to be drawn from this is not that we should despair of ever being able to distinguish good interpretations from bad. It is rather that we should not take it for granted, even in apparently quite straightforward cases, that we know what a given statement from our doctrinal past *meant*.

So far, in this chapter, we have concentrated on the problem of discontinuity between different cultural contexts. It does not follow that there has been no discernible continuity in christian belief and doctrine, but only that the work of discernment is often delicate and difficult. Having emphasised the discontinuities it is now incumbent upon us to indicate, in conclusion, where the element of doctrinal continuity in the process of tradition is to be sought.

In chapter 7, I suggested four factors making for continuity: the unchanging reference of christian doctrine to certain historical events; the pattern of the church's liturgical worship; the fact that the church has always been a structured community; and, fourthly, that there has been a continuity of christian meanings which was to be looked for, not so much in what has been *said* in the church at different periods, but rather in the concern or intention which had given rise to successive doctrinal statements. It is to that last suggestion that I would now like to return.

Not only has the terminology and meaning of dogmatic statements undergone considerable variation in the course of their history, but—as we have seen—the concept of 'dogma' itself has been subject to flux and variation. A statement such as 'dogmas do not change' seems to mean little more than that, from the standpoint of christian belief and a particular interpretation of the doctrine of divine providence, they remain permanent points of reference for christian faith and inquiry. At the end of a careful examination of doctrinal development in the patristic period, Maurice Wiles asks: 'If the continuity in the development of doctrine is not to be seen in a set of unchanging and unchangeable dogmas, where is it to be located? A partial answer, at least, might be that it is seen in a continuity of fundamental aims' (Wiles [1967] pp 171–172).

Wiles illustrates this suggestion from the recent history, in the catholic church, of teaching concerning religious liberty and birth-control (his book was written before the publication of *Humanae Vitae*): 'The kind of development which is postulated in each case is surely the kind for which we should be looking. The continuity is seen in the continuity of aim and objective' (p 173). He is aware of the fact that such a concept of continuity is compatible with radical shifts in doctrinal language and method: 'If we accept that development is to be understood in such terms, we cannot rule out in advance the possibility that it could involve shifts in doctrinal affirmation as radical as those embodied for science in the Copernican revolution or reversals of judgement as drastic as those envisaged in the case of religious liberty or (hypothetically) of contraception' (p 173). The suggestion here seems to be that even revolutionary change in the church's *affirmations* and practical judgements may be consistent with an underlying continuity in the question or challenge to which those affirmations respond. In order to pursue this suggestion, I shall make use of a remarkable (and, I think, neglected) study by George Vass.

His starting-point is impressively concrete: 'Anxiety, we are told by Kierkegaard, goes deeper than fear whose object we know. We may *fear* that new theories about the Eucharist, for example, falsify doctrine once defined, and weaken devotion. However, the suggestion that Christian truth is a changing, and thus a historical truth, not only on its surface but also in its entirety, seems to attack the very heart of our security in faith. Can we ever admit that with the changing context of the Church's life Christian truth is a changing truth, that it is not eternal but temporal?'(Vass [1968] p 130.)

As with many recent studies of the problem, Vass's articles have to be seen against the background of European debates on hermeneutics. Thus he assumes, from the outset, that christian truth is an *interpretation*. Any interpretation (here he seems to be following Gadamer) is the interpreter's answer to a question with which he has been confronted. Now, if we offer an interpretation of concrete, historical facts—eg, 'the political situation in this country threatens disaster' (p 276)—it might seem that the *truth* of our interpretation is to be assessed simply by comparing it with 'the facts'. In certain very straightforward cases, such as 'It is raining', this might work. In more complex cases, however, if the interpretation is to be a responsible, well-founded judgement, and not merely a random and ill-informed guess, the interpreter must be in possession of a wide range of skills. He must know, from personal experience, how to handle and evaluate evidence, how to employ criteria of relevance, how to test first one tentative solution, then another. Eventually, on the basis of that concrete, personal interpretative skill which Newman entitled the 'illative sense', he will recognise that one question rather than another is the key to the problem. His skill, as an interpreter, consists in his ability to detect the correct *question* to which his interpretation will be the response.

Therefore, if someone else wishes to test the validity, the truth of an interpretation, he has to get himself into a position in which he is able to ask the same question as the interpreter did. Only then is he able to say whether the interpretation was correct or incorrect, adequate or inadequate, true or false. Therefore, and this is the most original feature of Vass's contribution, the truth of an interpretation of concrete problems consists primarily in the correctness, the truth, of the *question* that is eventually asked, and only secondarily, and derivatively, in the truth of the answer provided (whether philosophers will be happy with the concept of truth-values attaching to questions, remains to be seen). 'I regard . . . Christian truth as an interpretation whose truth-value is primarily to be found in the questions it asks and secondarily in the answers it gives' (pp 279–280).

On this account, the christian's basic question is: 'Whether or not the meaning of human existence is to be worked out in view of the Christ event?' (p 280). What differentiates the christian from the non-christian is that the former is the man who, in the concrete, has been brought personally face-to-face with that question (albeit often in a very existential, unacademic, 'simple' way), and has answered: 'Yes'. The form of his response, his 'Yes', will be his confession of faith and a life lived in obedience to that commitment. In other words, although the answers which the church gives to the question about Christ, and to all the other questions which flow from it, may vary considerably from one historical and cultural context to another, the question to which they are forms of affirmative response is perennial and unchanging.

To suggest that the element of continuity in christian doctrine is to be sought at the level of the fundamental aims and objectives underlying confessional affirmation (Wiles), or in the questions to which that affirmation is the response (Vass), suggests a line of approach which, when thoroughly explored, would help to show that we are able to take with full seriousness the changes and discontinuities in doctrinal history without succumbing to a doctrinal relativism which would deprive the concept of ecclesial 'indefectibility' of any foundation in critical historical study. We must, however, go a step further and ask whether successive interpretations are merely successive, or whether there is not also an element of linearity, of irreversibility, of development, to be discerned in doctrinal history from within such a perspective.

In the first part of this chapter, we insisted on the importance of taking the stranger seriously as a stranger. Wolfhart Pannenberg, agreeing with Gadamer, makes the same point when he denies Bultmann's 'presupposition of a common self-

understanding between the author and the reader. Interpretation must first of all accept the strangeness of the text'
(Turner [1972] p 115). Pannenberg also accepts Gadamer's
demand 'that the interpreter ascertain the question to which
the text was an answer' (Pannenberg [1970a] p 122). But he
insists that 'talk about the "question" the text poses to us can
only be metaphorical: the text becomes a question only for
the one who asks questions' (pp 122–123). The danger of
employing the model of 'conversation', as Gadamer does, to
describe the hermeneutical process is that the relationship
between the text and the interpreter is conceived too 'inter-
subjectively'. That is to say, the risk is run of following Bultmann's path of escape from many of the problems of genuinely
historical understanding. Gadamer and Pannenberg both
refer to the 'horizons' within which the original author and
the later interpreter operate; both of them see the interpreter
as broadening, or changing his 'horizon' as he succeeds in
appropriating the 'horizon' of the original author. But Pannenberg lays the greater emphasis on the objectivity, the facticity,
of those historical events and historical assertions which alone
enable us to discover and appropriate the original author's
'world', or 'horizon', and thus to transform our own. (Significantly, the differences between them at this point is
closely connected with their different conceptions of revelation).

History, for Pannenberg, is the history of successive 'horizons', as these horizons have been expressed and enfleshed in
the events and 'monuments' of history. But the horizons are
not merely successive. The order of succession is important,
for if we are to understand assertions made within one 'horizon',
we must also understand the previous 'horizon' of which it is
the interpretation and development. Hence the emphasis
which he always lays on the concept of the 'transmission of
traditions'. He speaks of 'The historical process of the development and transmission of traditions, in the course of which the
unity of the man Jesus with God became recognised' (Pannenberg [1968] p 33). The understanding of this historical process is the task of dogmatics. It is thus not surprising that
Pannenberg should say that 'Dogmatics has an obligation to the
history of the church: a responsibility for the maintenance of

continuity with the tradition. The maintenance of this continuity has to do with protecting the unity of the church through time' (Pannenberg [1970c] p 208). Nevertheless, 'the church's dogma, which is still on the way, cannot itself be the eschatological form of revealed truth' (p 210).

'Any truth which claims to possess the key to history enslaves us. Only the truth which we seek in an encounter can make us free. And such is Christian truth: perennial in its quest for meaning, universally valid in the developing historical structure of its inevitable questions, at the same time it is a pilgrim on its way towards the fulfilment and conclusive evidence that it hopes to reach' (Vass [1968] p 289).

All that I have attempted to do in this chapter is to indicate two of the areas in which, on the basis of our contemporary experience and understanding of history, some of the questions usually discussed under the general rubric of doctrinal 'development' or 'evolution' might today appropriately be located. On the one hand, theologians would do well to keep in touch with practitioners in other disciplines, whose methodological problems significantly overlap with their own. On the other hand, we have seen in slightly more detail why it is that, according to Schillebeeckx, the problem of 'the "development of dogma"' . . . is the Catholic counterpart of what is known in Protestant theology as the "hermeneutical problem"' (Schillebeeckx [1969] p 6).

The problem of historical understanding and, in particular, the problem of discerning continuity across the discontinuities within cultural history, are common to many disciplines. But only theology is faced with the task of reconciling a full acceptance of the historical nature of human truth with the confession of christian faith that a word of eternal, imperishable truth and validity has been spoken in, and thus become part of the texture of our history. Both catholic and protestant theology have traditionally acknowledged the unique authority of the new testament as the privileged, because original, witness to that word made flesh. I should wish to assert that they must continue to do so. This assertion expresses an interpretation of history. As such, it is a rational act, which claims no immunity from historical criticism. But, as such, it is also in the last resort an irreducibly personal judgement; an expression of that concrete option which is christian belief. Similarly, I should wish to maintain that there are moments in the history of christian tradition when the church confesses its faith with peculiar decisiveness, confidence and clarity, and that the affirmations thus made remain—in different ways, and in varying degrees—normative for subsequent belief and exploration. In other words, I should wish to maintain that 'dogmatic statements' have been, and must be uttered. This assertion, too, expresses an interpretation of history. As such, it is a rational act, which claims no immunity from historical criticism. But, as such, it is also in the last resort an irreducibly personal judgement; a particular form of christian belief.

We have travelled some way from our examination of the first two chapters of *Dei Verbum* in part 1. But the same themes, the same problems, have been with us throughout. In conclusion, I would like to return to a suggestion that I made in chapter 7: namely, that if we are to seek for one 'model' which might enable us to hold together the myriad problems which attend our deeper awareness of the historical structure of christian truth, then there are few better candidates than the concept of *anamnesis*. In order to be obedient today, in word and action, to God's call to live for the promised future, the church must—in each concrete situation in which it finds itself— continually seek to remember its past. It must seek to remember its *entire* past, at least in the sense that, were any part of its history systematically to be excluded from the church's present memory, the result would be an impoverishment of the church's experience of that revelation of God which is made to it *in* that history, as the deepest meaning of that history.

This task of remembrance cannot be carried out from the standpoint of a detached or uncommitted observer. We have to take the risk of *using* the church's language, critically and responsibly, if we are to discover the past, and so learn to work in the direction of that human future which is promised to us in the new testament. There is no such thing as a common language 'which is not, at some point, based on a common life in which many individuals participate' (Winch [1970] p

33, following Wittgenstein). We have to learn to 'internalise [the] rules' of christian discourse, 'as socialised participants and not as impartial observers' (Habermas [1972] p 192).

'What keeps the church one and the same through all changes, however great, is that it always remembers certain specific historical events which culminate in Christ and continues to hope, not for just any kind of future, but for the definite future of the Lord's return' (Lindbeck [1968] p 117).

BIBLIOGRAPHY

Only works to which reference is made in this book are included.
For the sake of convenience, Newman's works are referred to in the text and notes by means of the abbreviations recommended by C. S. Dessain, *Letters and Diaries of John Henry Newman* xi (London 1961) pp xxv–xxvi.

Abbott, Walter M. ed *The Documents of Vatican II*. London 1966.

Bainvel, Jean V. *De Magisterio Vivo et Traditione*. Paris 1905.

Bakker, Leo. 'Man's Place in Divine Revelation' *Concilium* i, 3 (1967) 11–19.

Barmann, Lawrence F. *Baron Friedrich von Hügel and the Modernist Crisis in England*. Cambridge 1972.

Barth, Karl. *Church Dogmatics* i/1. Trans G. T. Thomson. Edinburgh 1936.

— 'Conciliorum Tridentini et Vatican i Inhaerens Vestigiis?' *Vatican II: La Révélation Divine* ii, 513–522. Trans J. Jegge. Paris 1968.

Baum, Gregory. 'Vatican II's Constitution on Revelation: History and Interpretation' *Theological Studies* xxviii (1967) 51–75.

— *The Credibility of the Church Today*. London 1968.

Beirnert, Wolfgang. 'The Ancient Creeds and New Brief Formulas' *International Catholic Review* (1972) 69–79.

Bent, Charles N. *Interpreting the Doctrine of God*. New York 1969.

Berger, Peter L. and Luckmann, Thomas. *The Social Construction of Reality*. London 1971.

Bergeron, Richard, *Les Abus de l'Eglise d'après Newman*. Tournai 1971.

Bévenot, Maurice. ' "Faith and Morals" in the Councils of Trent and Vatican i' *Heythrop Journal* iii (1962) 15–30.

— '*Traditiones* in the Council of Trent' *Heythrop Journal* iv (1963) 333–347.

— 'Primacy and Development' *Heythrop Journal* ix (1968) 400–413.

Blondel, Maurice. *L'Action. Essai d'une Critique de la Vie et d'une Science de la Pratique*. Paris 1893.

— '*De la Valeur Historique du Dogme*' *Les Premiers Ecrits de Maurice Blondel* ii, 229–245. Paris 1956.

— 'History and Dogma' *Maurice Blondel: The Letter on Apologetics and History and Dogma* 221–287. Ed Alexander Dru and Illtyd Trethowan. London, 1964.

184 BIBLIOGRAPHY

Bouyer, Louis. *L'Eucharistie: Théologie et Spiritualité de la Prière Eucharistique*. Tournai 1966.
Boyer, Charles. 'Qu'est-ce que la Théologie? Réflexions sur une Controverse' *Gregorianum* xxi (1940) 255–266.
Brekelmans, Antonius. 'Origin and Function of Creeds in the Early Church' *Concilium* i, 6 (1970) 33–42.
Brown, Raymond. 'The Virginal Conception of Jesus' *Theological Studies* xxxiii (1972) 3–34.
Bultmann, Rudolf. 'New Testament and Mythology' *Kerygma and Myth* i, 1–44. Ed H. W. Bartsch; trans Reginald H. Fuller. ²London 1964.
Butler, Basil Christopher. *The Theology of Vatican II*. London 1967.
Butler, Cuthbert. *The Vatican Council*. 2 vols, London 1930.
Butler, William Archer. *Letters on the Development of Christian Doctrine, in Reply to Mr Newman's Essay*. Ed Thomas Woodward. Dublin 1850.
Caprile, Giovanni. 'Trois Amendements au Schéma sur la Révélation' *Vatican II: La Révélation Divine* ii, 667–687. Paris 1968.
Chadwick, Owen. *From Bossuet to Newman: The Idea of Doctrinal Development*. Cambridge 1957.
— ed *The Mind of the Oxford Movement*. London 1960.
Collingwood, R. G. *The Idea of History*. Oxford 1946.
Concilium General Secretariat, eds. 'The Creed in the Melting-Pot' *Concilium* i, 6 (1970) 131–153.
Congar, Yves. *Tradition and Traditions*. Trans Michael Naseby and Thomas Rainborough. London 1966.
— [1970a]. 'Church History as a Branch of Theology' *Concilium* vii, 6 (1970) 85–96.
— [1970b]. *L'Eglise de Saint Augustin à l'Epoque Moderne*. Paris 1970.
— [1970c]. 'Infaillibilité et Indéfectibilité' *Revue des Sciences Philosophiques et Théologiques* liv (1970) 601–618.
Conzemius, Victor. 'Why Was the Primacy of the Pope Defined in 1870?' *Concilium* iv, 7 (1971) 75–83.
Coulson, John. 'Newman on the Church—His Final View, its Origin and Influence' *The Rediscovery of Newman: an Oxford Symposium* 123–143. Ed John Coulson and A. M. Allchin. London 1967.
— *Newman and the Common Tradition*. Oxford 1970.
Cullmann, Oscar. *The Earliest Christian Confessions*. Trans J. K. S. Reid. London 1949.
Davis, Henry Francis. 'Doctrine, Development of' *A Catholic Dictionary of Theology* ii, 177–189. London 1967.
Davison, John. *Discourses on Prophecy*. ⁷London 1861.

Denzinger, H. and Rahner, Karl, eds. *Enchiridion Symbolorum Definitionum et Declarationum de Rebus Fidei et Morum.* ³¹Rome 1957.

Dulles, Avery. 'Dogma as an Ecumenical Problem' *Theological Studies* xxix (1968) 397–416.

Dupuy, Bernard -D. 'Historique de la Constitution' *Vatican II: La Révélation Divine* i, 61–117. Paris 1968.

Echlin, E. P. 'Foreword' to *Spirit, Faith, and Church* by Wolfhart Pannenberg, Avery Dulles and Carl E. Braaten. Philadelphia 1970.

Feyerabend, Paul K. 'Consolations for the Specialist' *Criticism and the Growth of Knowledge* 197–230. Ed Imre Lakatos and Alan Musgrave. Cambridge 1970.

Foucault, Michael. *The Archeology of Knowledge,* trans A. M. Sheridan Smith. London 1972.

Fransen, Piet F. 'Unity and Confessional Statements: Historical and Theological Inquiry of R. C. Traditional Conceptions' *Bijdragen* xxx (1972) 2–38.

Gadamer, H. G. *Wahrheit und Methode.* Tübingen 1960.

Geiselmann, R. *Die Heilige Schrift und Die Tradition.* Fribourg 1962.

Gellner, Ernest. 'Concepts and Society' *Rationality* 18–49. Ed Bryan S. Wilson. Oxford 1970.

Groot, J. C. 'Aspects Horizontaux de la Collégialité' *L'Eglise de Vatican II* iii, 805–828. Ed G. Barauna and Y. Congar. Paris 1966.

Habermas, Jurgen. *Knowledge and Human Interests.* Trans Jeremy J. Shapiro. London 1972.

Hammans, Herbert. 'Recent Catholic Views on the Development of Dogma' *Concilium* i, 3 (1967) 53–63.

Hanson, R. P. C. *Tradition in the Early Church.* London 1962.

Harent, S. 'Modernisme, I Partie: Le Décret "Lamentabili Sane Exitu"; III: Eglise et Sacraments' *Dictionnaire d'Apologétique et de la Foi Catholique* iii, cols 606–618. Ed A. D'Alès. Paris 1909.

Harnack, Adolf. *What is Christianity?* Trans T. B. Saunders. London 1901.

Harris, Peter and others. *On Human Life: An Examination of Humanae Vitae.* London 1968.

Harvey, V. A. *The Historian and the Believer.* London 1967.

Heaney, J. J. *The Modernist Crisis: Von Hügel.* Washington 1968.

Hesse, Mary B. 'Hermeticism and Historiography: An Apology for the Internal History of Science', *Minnesota Studies in the Philosophy of Science.* v *Historical and Philosophical Perspectives of Science* 134–160. Ed Roger H. Stuewer. Minneapolis 1970.

Holmes, J. Derek. 'Cardinal Newman and the First Vatican Council' *Annuarium Historiae Conciliorum*. Ed W. Brandmüller and R. Bäumer. i, 2 (1969) 374–398.
— 'Cardinal Newman on the Philosophy of History' *Tijdschrift voor Filosofie* xxxiii (1970) 521–535.
von Hügel, Friedrich. 'The Church and the Bible: The Two Stages of their Inter-Relation' *Dublin Review* cxv (1894) 313–341.
Hughes, John Jay. 'Infallible? An Inquiry Considered' *Theological Studies* xxxii (1971) 183–207.
Jossua, Jean-Pierre. 'Immutabilité, Progrès ou Structurations Multiples des Doctrines Chrétiennes' *Revue des Sciences Philosophiques et Théologiques* lii (1968) 173–200.
— 'Rule of Faith and Orthodoxy' *Concilium* i, 6 (1970) 56–67.
— 'Signification des Confessions de Foi' *Istina* xvii (1972) 48–56.
Kasper, Walter. 'The Relationship Between Gospel and Dogma: An Historical Approach' *Concilium* i, 3 (1967) 73–79.
Kelly, J. N. D. *Early Christian Creeds*. ²London 1960.
Kuhn, Thomas S. *The Structure of Scientific Revolutions*. Chicago 1962.
— 'Reflections on My Critics' *Criticism and the Growth of Knowledge* 231–278. Ed Imre Lakatos and Alan Musgrave. Cambridge 1970.
Küng, Hans. *Infallible? An Enquiry*. Trans Eric Mosbacher. London 1971.
Lash, Nicholas L. A. *His Presence in the World*. London 1968.
— 'The Notions of "Implicit" and "Explicit" Reason in Newman's University Sermons: A Difficulty' *Heythrop Journal* xi (1970) 48–54.
— [1971a]. 'Development of Doctrine: Smokescreen or Explanation?' *New Blackfriars* lii (1971) 101–108.
— [1971b]. 'Faith and History: Some Reflections on Newman's "Essay on the Development of Christian Doctrine"' *Irish Theological Quarterly* xxxviii (1971) 224–241.
— [1971c]. 'De Ontwikkeling van het Geloofsdenken' *Tijdschrift voor Theologie* xi (1971) 52–65.
— 'Credal Affirmation as a Criterion of Church Membership', *Intercommunion and Church Membership* 51–73. Ed John Kent and Robert Murray. London 1973.
Lease, Gary. *Witness to the Faith: Cardinal Newman on the Teaching Authority of the Church*. Shannon 1971.
Lengsfeld, Peter. 'La Tradition dans le Temps Constitutif de la Révélation' *Mysterium Salutis: Dogmatique de l'Histoire du Salut* i/2, 11–68. Paris 1969.

Le Roy, Edouard. *What is a Dogma?* Chicago 1918.

Leuba, Jean-Louis. 'La Tradition à Montréal et à Vatican II: Convergences et Questions' *Vatican II: La Révélation Divine* ii, 475–497. Paris 1968.

Lindbeck, George A. 'The Problem of Doctrinal Development and Contemporary Protestant Theology' *Concilium* i, 3 (1967) 64–72.

— 'The Framework of Catholic-Protestant Disagreement' *The Word in History* 102–119. Ed T. P. Burke. London 1968.

— *The Future of Roman Catholic Theology*. London 1970.

[Loisy, Alfred Firmin]. A. Firmin. 'Le Développement Chrétien d'après le Cardinal Newman' *Revue du Clergé Francais* xvii (1898) 5–20.

[—] [1899a]. 'La Théorie Individualiste de la Religion', *Revue du Clergé Francais* xvii (1899) 202–215.

[—] [1899b]. 'La Définition de la Religion' *Revue du Clergé Francais* xviii (1899) 193–209.

[—] [1900a]. 'L'Idée de la Révélation' *Revue du Clergé Francais* xxi (1900) 250–271.

[—] [1900b]. 'Les Preuves et l'Economie de la Révélation' *Revue du Clergé Francais* xxii (1900) 126–153.

[—] [1900c]. 'La Religion d'Israel' *Revue du Clergé Francais* xxiv (1900) 337–363.

[—] *L'Evangile et l'Eglise*. Paris 1902.

— *Autour d'un Petit Livre*. Paris 1903.

— *Simples Réflexions sur le Décret du Saint-Office 'Lamentabili Sane Exitu' et sur l'Encyclique 'Pascendi Dominici Gregis'*. Privately printed 1908.

Lonergan, Bernard J. F. *Insight: A Study of Human Understanding*. London 1957.

— *Divinarum Personarum Conceptio Analogica*. ²Rome 1959.

— [1967a]. *Collection*. London 1967.

— [1967b]. 'The Dehellenization of Dogma' *Theological Studies* xxviii (1967) 336–351.

— 'Theology in its New Context' *Theology of Renewal. 1. Renewal of Religious Thought* 34–46. Ed L. K. Shook. New York 1968.

— 'Bernard Lonergan Responds' *Foundations of Theology* 223–234. Ed Philip McShane. Dublin 1971.

— [1972a]. *Method in Theology*. London 1972.

— [1972b]. 'The Response of the Jesuit, as Priest and Apostle, in the Modern World' *Nova et Vetera*. Privately printed for the members of the Society of the Divine Word 1972.

de Lubac, Henri. 'Bulletin de Théologie Fondamentale: Le

Problème du Développement du Dogme' *Recherches de Science Religieuse* xxxv (1948) 130–160.
— 'Commentaire du Préambule et du Chapitre 1' *Vatican* II: *La Révélation Divine* i, 157–302. Paris 1968.
— *La Foi Chrétienne: Essai sur la Structure du Symbole des Apôtres.* Paris 1969.
McGrath, Mark G. *The Vatican Council's Teaching on the Evolution of Dogma.* Rome 1953.
McKenzie, John L. *Dictionary of the Bible.* London 1966.
MacKinnon, E. 'Humanae Vitae *and Doctrinal Development' Continuum* vi, 2 (1968).
Mackey, James P. *The Modern Theology of Tradition.* London 1962.
Marin-Sola, F. *L'Evolution Homogène du Dogme Catholique.* 2 vols Fribourg 1924.
Maurice, Frederick Denison. *The Epistle to the Hebrews.* London 1846.
Meulenberg, Leonardus. 'Gregory VII and the Bishops: Centralization of Power?' *Concilium* i, 8 (1972) 65–78.
Minear, Paul S. 'A Protestant Point of View' *Vatican* II: *An Interfaith Appraisal* 68–88 Ed John H. Miller. Notre Dame 1966.
Misner, Paul. 'Newman's Concept of Revelation and the Development of Doctrine' *Heythrop Journal* xi (1970) 32–47.
Moore, Sebastian. *God is a New Language.* London 1967.
Moran, Gabriel. *Theology of Revelation.* London 1967.
Murray, Robert. 'Newman's Place in the Development of the Catholic Doctrine of Inspiration' *John Henry Newman: On the Inspiration of Scripture* 48–96. Ed J. Derek Homes and Robert Murray. London 1967.
— 'Who or What is Infallible?' *Infallibility in the Church: An Anglican-Catholic Dialogue* 26–46. London 1968.
Newman, John Henry. [Apo] *Apologia Pro Vita Sua.* London 1873.
— [Ari]. *The Arians of the Fourth Century.* London 1897.
— [—] [1836]. 'The Brothers Controversy: Apostolical Tradition' *British Critic* xx (1836) 166–199.
— [Diff I, II]. *Certain Difficulties Felt by Anglicans in Catholic Teaching.* 2 vols London 1918, 1920.
— [D.A.]. *Discussions and Arguments on Various Subjects.* London 1872.
— [G.A.]. *An Essay in Aid of a Grammar of Assent.* London 1889.
— [Dev]. *An Essay on the Development of Christian Doctrine.* [3]London 1878.
— [Ess I, II]. *Essays Critical and Historical.* 2 vols London 1919.
— [U.S.]. *Fifteen Sermons Preached Before the University of Oxford.* London 1892.

— [H.S. I, II, III]. *Historical Sketches.* 3 vols London 1872.
— [L&D XI–XXII]. *The Letters and Diaries of John Henry Newman.* Ed Charles Stephen Dessain. 12 vols (XI–XXII) to date. London 1961–1972.
— [P.S. I–VIII]. *Parochial and Plain Sermons.* 8 vols London 1868.
— [S.D.]. *Sermons Bearing on Subjects of the Day.* London 1869.
— [V.M. I, II]. *The Via Media of the Anglican Church.* 2 vols London 1891.
O'Donovan, Leo J. 'Lonergan: Emergent Probability and Evolution' *Continuum* vii (1969).
Pannenberg, Wolfhart. *Jesus—God and Man.* Trans Lewis L. Wilkins and Duane A. Priebe. London 1968.
— [1970a]. 'Hermeneutic and Universal History', *Basic Questions in Theology* i, 96–136. Trans George H. Kehm. London 1970.
— [1970b]. 'Redemptive Event and History' *Basic Questions in Theology* i, 15–80. Trans Shirley C. Guthrie and George H. Kehm. London 1970.
— [1970c]. 'What is a Dogmatic Statement?' *Basic Questions in Theology* i, 182–210. Trans George H. Kehm. London 1970.
Pelikan, Jaroslav. *Development of Christian Doctrine.* London 1969.
— *Historical Theology: Change and Continuity in Christian Doctrine.* London 1971.
Petit L. and Martin J. B., eds *Collectio Conciliorum Recentiorum Ecclesiae Universae* xiv. Arnhem 1924. (Mansi, L).
Popper, Karl. 'Normal Science and its Dangers' *Criticism and the Growth of Knowledge* 51–58. Ed Imre Lakatos and Alan Musgrave. Cambridge 1970.
Poulat, Emil. *Histoire, Dogme et Critique dans la Crise Moderniste.* Paris 1962.
— 'Critique Historique et Théologie dans la Crise Moderniste' *Recherches de Science Religieuse* lviii (1970) 535–550.
Pozo, Candido. 'Development of Dogma' *Sacramentum Mundi* ii, 98–102. New York 1968.
Rahner, Karl. [1961a]. 'The Development of Dogma' *Theological Investigations* i, 39–77. Trans Cornelius Ernst. London 1961.
— [1961b]. 'The Immaculate Conception' *Theological Investigations* i, 201–213. Trans Cornelius Ernst. London 1961.
— [1961c]. 'The Interpretation of the Dogma of the Assumption' *Theological Investigations* i, 215–227. Trans Cornelius Ernst. London 1961.
— [1963]. 'Forgotten Truths Concerning the Sacrament of Penance' *Theological Investigations* ii, 135–174. Trans Karl-H. Kruger. London 1963.

— [1966a]. 'Considerations on the Development of Dogma' *Theological Investigations* iv, 3–35. Trans Kevin Smyth. London 1966.
— [1966b]. 'Theology in the New Testament' *Theological Investigations* v, 23–41. Trans Karl-H. Kruger. London 1966.
— [1967]. 'The Dogma of the Immaculate Conception in our Spiritual Life' *Theological Investigations* iii, 129–140. Trans Karl-H. and Boniface Kruger. London 1967.
— [1969a] and Lehmann, Karl. 'Historicité de la Transmission' *Mysterium Salutis: Dogmatique de l'Histoire du Salut* i/3, 313–386. Paris 1969.
— [1969b] and Lehmann, Karl. 'Kérygme et Dogme' *Mysterium Salutis* i/3, 183–280. Paris 1969.
— [1969c] 'Pluralism in Theology and the Unity of the Church's Confession of Faith' *Concilium* vi, 5 (1969) 49–58.
Ratzinger, Joseph. 'On the Interpretation of the Tridentine Decree on Tradition' *Revelation and Tradition* 50–68, by Karl Rahner and Joseph Ratzinger. Trans W. J. O'Hara. New York 1966.
Reardon, Bernard M. G. ed. *Roman Catholic Modernism*. London 1970.
Richard, Robert L. 'Contribution to a Theory of Doctrinal Development' *Spirit as Inquiry: Studies in Honour of Bernard Lonergan* 205–227. *Continuum* ii, 3. Ed F. E. Crowe (1964).
Rynne, Xavier. *Letters from Vatican City*. London 1963.
— *The Third Session*. London 1965.
— *The Fourth Session*. London 1966.
Schillebeeckx, Edward. *Revelation and Theology*. Trans N. D. Smith. London 1967.
— *God the Future of Man*. Trans N. D. Smith. London 1969.
Schlink, Edmund. 'The Structure of Dogmatic Statements as an Ecumenical Problem' *The Coming Christ and the Coming Church* 16–84. Trans G. Overlach and D. B. Simmonds. Edinburgh 1967.
Schoof, Mark. *Breakthrough: The Beginnings of the New Catholic Theology*. Trans N. D. Smith. Dublin 1970.
Schoonenberg, Piet. 'Historicity and the Interpretation of Dogma' *Theology Digest* xviii (1970) 132–143.
Simonin, H. D. 'La Théologie Thomiste de la Foi et le Développement du Dogme' *Revue Thomiste* xviii (1935) 537–556.
Spencer, Herbert. *Essays on Education and Kindred Subjects*. London 1966.
Stern, Jean. *Bible et Tradition chez Newman*. Paris 1967.

Tavard, George. *Holy Writ or Holy Church*. London 1959.
— 'Commentary on *De Revelatione*' *Journal of Ecumenical Studies* iii (1966) 1–35.
Thils, Gustave. *L'Infaillibilité Pontificale: Sources—Conditions—Limites*. Gembloux 1969.
Thurian, Max. [1968a]. 'Renewal and the Scripture-Tradition Problem in the Light of Vatican II and Montreal 1963' *Theology of Renewal: 1 Renewal of Religious Thought* 66–82. Ed L. K. Shook. New York 1968.
— [1968b] and Schutz, Roger. *Revelation: A Protestant View*. Westminster, Maryland 1968.
Tillich, Paul. *Perspectives on Nineteenth and Twentieth Century Protestant Theology*. London 1967.
Toulmin, Stephen. *The Uses of Argument*. Cambridge 1964.
Turner, Geoffrey. 'Wolfhart Pannenberg and the Hermeneutical Problem' *Irish Theological Quarterly* xxxix (1972) 107–129.
Van Leeuwen, Peter, 'The Genesis of the Constitution on Divine Revelation' *Concilium* i, 3 (1967) 4–10.
Van Ruler, A. A. 'The Evolution of Dogma' *Christianity Divided* 89–105. Ed Daniel J. Callahan, Heiko Obermann, Daniel J. O'Hanlon. London 1961.
Vass, George. 'On the Historical Structure of Christian Truth' *Heythrop Journal* ix (1968) 129–142, 274–289.
da Veiga Coutinho, L. *Tradition et Histoire dans la Controverse Moderniste (1898–1910)*. Rome 1954.
Venards, Louis. 'La Valeur Historique du Dogme' *Bulletin de Littérature Ecclésiastique de Toulouse* v (1904) 338–357.
Vidler, Alec. *The Modernist Movement in the Roman Church*. Cambridge 1934.
— *A Variety of Catholic Modernists*. Cambridge 1970.
Walgrave, Jan-H. *Unfolding Revelation: The Nature of Doctrinal Development*. London 1972.
Ward, Maisie. *The Wilfrid Wards and the Transition*. II *Insurrection versus Resurrection*. London 1937.
Wiles, Maurice. *The Making of Christian Doctrine*. Cambridge 1967.
Willam, Franz Michel. *Der Erkenntnislehre Kardinal Newmans*. Frankfurt 1969.
Winch, Peter. *The Idea of a Social Science*. London 1970.
Zahrnt, Heinz. *The Question of God*. Trans R. A. Wilson. London 1969.

INDEX

194   INDEX

Conzemius, V., 77
Coulson, J., 101, 127n
Creed, 46–57 *passim*, 95, 155ff
    Apostles', 94ff, 155, 159, 161f
    as act of worship, 47f, 50, 52,
        157–9
    as confessional formula, 39, 46–
        50, 52–3, 159
    as dogma, 51, 158–9, 165
    Athanasian, 50, 88, 155
    'Creed of Pius IV', 88, 155
    'doctrinal creeds', 49f, 51, 88,
        151, 155, 159f
    Nicene, 50, 151, 155, 159, 161
Cullmann, O., 58n

DAVIS, H. F., 94
Davison, J., 93
Development,
    and biological or organic analo-
        gies, 39, 53, 56, 94f, 113, 119,
        133, 138, 145, 148
    and discontinuity, 26f, 61, 138,
        149, 153, 175, 178
    and fulfilment of prophecy, 93
    and the Holy Spirit, 26, 61, 69
    as 'expansion', 132, 145
    as 'explanation', 66
    as interpretation, 66, 93, 110
    by 'pruning', 145ff, 152
    cumulative, 28, 130ff, 169
    linear, 16, 28, 61f, 94, 144f, 148f,
        178
    'logical' and 'theological' theo-
        ries of, 120, 123–5, 127n, 128f
    psychological analogies for, 93,
        130, 132
    through 'demolition', 135, 146f,
        152
Doctrine, *see* Dogma, Dogmatic
    statements
Dogma, 46–57, 156f, 176
    and 'infallibility' (qv), 57, 76–9
    at Council of Trent, 53–4
    biblical uses of term, 46f
    'irreformability' of, 36, 56f, 66,
        74, 76–9 *passim*, 95, 107, 109,
        120, 134, 139, 154

patristic uses of term, 47
permanence of, 65–6
univocal concept of, 165
Dogmatic statements,
    and historical facticity, 60, 124,
        159–60
    as christological statements, 48,
        162, 164–5
    as propositional, 130, 156f
    as symbolic, 49, 51f, 85, 105,
        155ff, 163
    criteria for classification, 79,
        156–9, 161–5
    doctrinal or interpretative func-
        tion of, 66, 158ff, 163, 165f
    doxological function of, 47f, 50,
        52ff, 157–9, 163, 165
    inadequacy of, 56, 60, 105, 109,
        131
    liturgical context of, 159f
    negative or protective function
        of, 62, 105, 159f, 163, 165f
    unity of, 134, 155, 160, 162, 164
Dulles, A., 160
Dupuy, B. D., 6, 9n, 29, 30

ECHLIN, E. P., 94
Epistemé, 166
    epistemic shift, 51–2, 67, 83,
        144f, 148, 153, 154n, 166,
        168f
    epistemological perspectives, 37,
        83, 112
Essence of christianity, 106, 109ff,
    119
    as 'germ' or 'kernel', 105–6, 126,
        145ff, 166
Eucharist, 65, 67–8, 160, 177
    eucharistic doctrine, 163
    eucharistic prayers, 48
Evolution,
    and development, 16–17, 61–2,
        113, 120, 168, 180
    and progress, 28f, 119, 138,
        148f
    'homogeneous', 17, 94, 119, 120–
        2, 130, 133, 144, 152, 169
Extrinsicism, 114